One Step at a Time

Memoir of a Former Quadriplegic

I0624107

Michael McCord

Tributes

What I loved most about this book was Mike's courage, endurance, and perseverance during these perilous times.

There was nothing I disliked about this book. It was inspiring as he was able to touch the lives of various quadriplegics, including Mark, who was as determined as Mike was to do the impossible and walk again. Although I found a few grammatical errors while reading, it was exciting and not tedious at any point in my reading process.

I would rate the book **5 out of 5 stars** because it was educative, inspiring, and intriguing to read. I would also state that it is professionally edited because I only found a few grammatical errors while reading it.

I would recommend One Step at a Time: Memoir of a Former Quadriplegic to victims of quadriplegic accidents and also to individuals who are feeling down and think everything isn't going as planned for them in this world. This book is inspiring and serves as motivation for readers who are doubting their potential.

Jay David Randall

OnlineBookClub.org

19 Jan 2023

"A quarter million Americans have spinal cord injuries, nearly half of whom are quadriplegic. My wish for each of them is that they have a copy of Mike McCord's *One Step at a Time,* his inspiring account of his journey from quadriplegia to climbing mountains. Mike's experience is one of enduring courage, hope, faith, and the eventual dedication of his life to serving others. If you are troubled physically, psychologically, or spiritually, this triumphant account will help you soar. Mike reminds us that, although tragedies happen, so does healing: a lesson we must never forget."

Larry Dossey, MD

Author: *One Mind: How Our Individual Mind Is Part of a Greater Consciousness and Why It Matters*

"Mike McCord's story is the triumphant overcoming, against all odds, of numerous setbacks, any one of which would have stopped a lesser spirit. He stands as an inspiration to the rest of us who have dealt with only a fraction of the adversity over which he has been victorious. I count him as a role model and a friend. Read his story and let him lift you up."

Gregory Barrette,

Vice President, International New Thought Alliance and Unity Minister

"Mike McCord is a true inspiration. His book is a poignant merging of science, spirituality, and positive thinking – a roadmap to overcoming obstacles and creating miracles that apply to each of us."

Connie "Crash" Humiston, Evolving Magazine

Library of Congress Cataloguing-in-Publication Data McCord, Michael L., One Step at a Time, Memoir of a Former Quadriplegic – 1st edition, rev.

ISBN- : 978-1-965384-56-5

LCCN: 2014916990

BISAC: Self-Help / Motivational & Inspirational.

Disclaimer

In this, the revised edition of "One Step at a Time," readers are invited to delve into an enhanced narrative, offering fresh insights and immersive experiences. This republished version introduces additional elements and refinements, providing both new and returning readers with an enriched reading adventure.

Table of Contents

Acknowledgments

To all the angels – living and beyond – who came to my aid during my darkest hours.

Johnson County, Kansas Med-Act Team; Overland Park Regional Hospital Emergency Care Unit, Overland Park, Kansas; Unity Church of Overland Park and Unity Worldwide Ministries; and The Rehabilitation Institute, Kansas City, Missouri.

Dr. Christopher Anderson; Rev. Greg Barrette; Dr. Robert Beatty, Neurosurgeon; Cindy Kottmeyer Botham; Dr. Patrick Caffrey; Allan Creek, M.D.; Cathy DeVriess, Occupational Therapist, Joseph Gardner; Tony Haggler; Karen Harrison; Pat Huard, PhD; Rev. Nancy Jerome; Jane Hart, Spiritual Counselor; Warren Kurtz, Reiki Master; Dr. John L'Ecuyer, PhD; Randy Leighton, Physical Therapist; Jean McCord; Les McCord; Rod McCord; Ryan McCord; Sean McCord; Brad & Diane Masters, Reiki Masters; Kay Ornella; Mary Roy; Paul Shall, Physical Therapist; Monica Schaal and "Steen," Nurse's Aides.

I also want to thank Darby, my Boston Terrier, for being my truest, unfailing friend and companion at a time when I needed one the most. I will always love and miss you.

Lastly, I want to thank my ex-wife, Cindy. We shared 30 years of our lives together and, although there were many difficult times there also were many good ones. She supported me during the most challenging period of our lives and stayed with me until I had mostly recovered from my injury and secured a permanent job.

Foreword

An old Hindu legend tells us that long ago, all human beings were once gods. However, when they abused their powers, Brahma, the great Lord of all the gods, decided to take back their divinity and hide it where it would never be found. The problem was where to find such a hiding place.

A council of gods was formed to help solve the problem. In time, they came up with the following suggestions:

- Let us bury the divinity of human beings deep in the ground. But Brahma replied, no, that won't do because sooner or later it will be dug up and found.
- Another god proposed: Let us throw it into the depths of the deepest ocean. But Brahma replied, no, that won't do because sooner or later they will explore the depths of all the oceans, and one day they will find it and bring it to the surface.

Eventually, Brahma shook his head and said, I know a place where they will never think to look. We shall hide the divinity of human beings in the deepest depths of themselves, for it is the only place where they will never look.

> I am responsible for what I see.
> I choose the feelings I experience,
> and I decide
> Upon the goal I would achieve.
> And everything that seems to happen to me I ask for,
> and receive as I have asked.
> *A Course in Miracles*
> Text, Ch 21, II

"If you always put limits on everything you do, physical or anything else, it will spread into your work and into your life. There are no limits, there are only plateaus and you must not stay there, you must go beyond them."--Bruce Lee

https://www.brainyquote.com

Preface

Since the original publication of *One Step at a Time, Memoir of a Former Quadriplegic* in 2015, life has thrown more curves my way. They have enabled me to gain new insights into the connection between mind and body.

Between 2015 and 2017, I had bouts of Rocky Mountain Spotted Fever, the first of which kept me in the hospital for 29 days, including two trips to the ICU. This was followed by hand surgery that was botched by the surgeon, two rotator cuff tears caused by falling, and, most recently, two knee replacements. These things slowed me, but only temporarily.

In 2020, I retired following a career in urban redevelopment, commercial real estate lending, environmental management, and as a commercial real estate review appraiser for the Department of Housing and Urban Development. My lifelong commitment to protecting the environment continues as team leader of Unity Worldwide Ministries' EarthCare Ministry. I also remain a genealogist as well as a field investigator for the Mutual UFO Network (MUFON).

Mentorship through the Christopher Reeve Foundation continues, although most of my assistance has come from outside the organization. In 2020, I taught a six-week class entitled "Healing and Wholeness" for Friends of Unity, Plymouth, MI. The course taught the difference between the two.

My quest for understanding the power each of us possesses to manifest our desires remains unabated, including additional scientific evidence that supports its existence. Much of this is contained in the revised Epilogue.

By way of review, in a span of 18 months between 2001 and 2003, I suffered three calamitous life-altering events: paralysis, job loss, and divorce.

The paralysis was the result of a fall at home that broke my neck (C-5) and damaged my spinal cord. I was left quadriplegic with about a 10% chance of ever walking again, according to both my neurosurgeon and physical therapist. Five months later, I was laid off from my job with a major banking institution. Lastly, in 2003 my wife of 30 years divorced me.

These events shook my soul, and it would have been easy to give up. But this wasn't in my nature. While the book chronicles my journey through these traumatic events, it also highlights my life from age four to 51. Each episode is a short story filled with lessons that, brick by brick, lay the foundation for characteristics that later proved to be vitally important. Among these is a moral received at age four, childhood through adolescence, college, marriage, and an up-and-down career filled with karmic implications.

The story also chronicles my journey to understand more about the "how and why" of the universe, as well as my spiritual growth from agnosticism toward spiritual enlightenment, a process that continues to this day. So it is, in fact, a lesson book of what I learned and how the reader may use my experiences to overcome challenges in their own lives.

By weaving scientific principles with fundamental spiritual teachings, the interconnectedness between the two is shown as well as the power each person has to manifest their own destiny. This "secret science behind miracles" has profound implications far beyond the body's physical healing. Through it, I achieved things not many thought possible, and so can you!

All of our lives comprise rocky roads filled with many twists and turns, ups and downs, heartbreaks, and joys. While we know "stuff" happens, the question is, how do we respond? It is my hope that the reader will be able to use the things I learned to create their own roadmap to recovery.

In spite of the many curves life has thrown at me, I continue to see the positive side of life. So should you! Nothing and no one can take away your ability to determine the way you view every situation and reclaim your right to health and happiness. The old adage is true, the only limitations you have are those you place upon yourself.

Mike McCord
August 24, 2024

Prologue

Tick, Tock, Tick Tock, Tick Tock.....

The second hand of my bedside clock marched methodically on its endless journey around the dial one fall day. The house was quiet except for the gentle stir of the curtains in the bedroom window. Outside, newly fallen leaves rustled in the fall breeze, whispering a reminder of frigid times to come.

Dreamily, I watched the seconds go by. My thoughts meandered among things important to an eight-year-old: what will we do at Scouts this week? The encyclopedia ships Robbie, and I are tracing sure are cool. I can't wait to play football in Tim's backyard next weekend.

Eventually, I looked back at the clock. As I pondered each tick, it dawned on me that each second was a unique moment that lasted for only the briefest of instants and then was gone forever. Although each second seemed insignificant, it was the only real thing in the world.

What would happen in my life to fill all my future ticks? What would I do with my life? Where would I live? Who would I become? Maybe I'd become a professional baseball player. Or maybe do something meaningful for humanity and get my name in the encyclopedia. The possibilities were endless, and nothing seemed impossible or beyond my reach.

On that warm afternoon so long ago, I never could have fathomed the amazing things that life had in store for me. Little did I know what a wild ride it was going to be!

Chapter 1
I Think I Can

I was SO excited! I loved the new record Santa Claus had brought me, "The Little Engine That Could." I loved the story about the little train that no one gave a chance of being anything more than a forgotten switch engine in the railroad yard. But the little engine believed in herself, even if no one else did. One day, a big locomotive pulling a train of toys over a tall mountain broke down, and the train sat stranded. The dolls and toys pleaded, but no other engine would help. Finally, the tiny engine came by, and in desperation, they asked her if she would help. Despite initial doubts, the little engine agreed to give it a try. She hitched herself to the long, heavy train and strained to make it move. At first, the train wouldn't budge, but she kept trying until slowly, very slowly, the train inched forward. The small engine groaned and strained to keep the heavy load moving. Eventually, the train picked up speed. Then they came to the tall mountain, the most challenging thing the little engine had done. As the train crept up the mountain, the little engine kept saying to herself, "I think I can, I think I can." Ultimately, against all odds and everyone's belief but her own, the train made it to the top of the mountain. All the toys cheered! And as the train started down the mountain, the little engine said to herself, "I knew I could, I knew I Could, I knew I could!"[1]

Oh, how I admired the courage and willpower of the little engine that no one believed in but her. Over and over, I played the record until it finally wore out. But the words seared into my soul: "I think I can, I think I can!"

Now eight years old, I whispered, "Hey Rod, I think there are buffaloes over that hill. Be quiet, or they'll hear us." We crept to the top of the hill, keeping close to the short bluestem growing around our pasture. At the top of the hill, we raised our heads to look around: a herd of Herefords munched grass at the bottom of the hill. No matter. To us, they were buffaloes, and we were scouts with Kit Carson exploring the Great American Desert.

1

Sun stripes chased the buffalo over the next hill while blue-green shafts of little-stem prairie grass undulated lazily in the wind. Golden fields of grain could be seen in distant fields, all of which were overarched by an endlessly blue sky.

While life was monotonous, predictable and at times dull in our little town of Nelson in southern Nebraska, with a population of 714, to me, it was exciting. Some of the images burned in my Nebraska soul include:

- Sudden violent thunderstorms accompanied by hail, lightning, and high winds.
- Tornado warnings that filled our hearts with fear. Sometimes the fear was realized.
- Raging blizzards howling unchecked across the treeless plains.
- The wind whistling through my hair as I sped down gravel streets on my bike.
- Exploring sun-kissed prairie oceans, hidden glens, and tree-lined creeks that encroached to the very edge of our little hamlet. Reveling in the freedom, security, and naivete of our secluded little corner of the world.

Still, it was a timeless "Rockwellan" existence. Both sides of my family had settled in Nebraska before 1870 and were pioneers in every sense of the word. Life was hard, even treacherous, and only those with enough courage, stamina, and determination survived. I was proud to carry their genes.

My family moved to Nelson in 1956 from Superior, a slightly larger Nebraska town 12 miles away, where my parents managed a grocery store owned by my uncle, Russ McCord. Three years later, their hard work paid off, and they bought the grocery store outright and renamed it the "Nelson Food Center." Both Mom and Dad came from large, poor families and hadn't been given much of a start in life. Dad had to quit school after the eighth grade to work on the farm, while Mom was told to leave home at age 18 as it was time for her to get out on her own. Now, they had created an opportunity where there had been none before. They were a terrific team with a winning formula that made the business successful for the next 35 years.

While we had several employees, every family member was expected to work at our store and do their share. There wasn't a lot of money, but the business always provided enough for us to get by with a little left over. We were a happy family, sustained by the idea that things would turn out in the long run if you worked hard and played fair.

As childhood turned into puberty, I became very hard on myself. Night after night, my 16-year-old self would lay awake until the wee hours of the morning, berating myself as destructive thoughts from somewhere deep inside bubbled to the surface. Over and over, night after night, I pounded negative self-concepts into my head until it scarred my soul. I drew deep within myself and was later dubbed "the silent senior" in the high school annual. My self-inflicted psychological wounds would take decades to heal.

In spite of my shyness, everyone liked me, and I had a close circle of friends. Being a decent athlete in baseball and football also helped win people over.

Finally, the day for high school graduation came! In May of 1968, one of the most tumultuous years in the 20th century, I was 18 years old. It was the height of the Vietnam War, a time of madness that grew into a movement challenging traditional values and mores. My generation believed the coming "Age of Aquarius" was dawning upon a new world in which all things were possible. While our generation did change many things, the beautiful vision was marred by violence, tragedy, and sadness—from the assassinations of Martin Luther King and Bobbie Kennedy to the "police riot" at the Democratic Convention in Chicago to the mindless killings committed by Charles Manson and his family. Meanwhile, the Vietnam War seemed to escalate daily. The world seemed to have turned upside down.

That fall, I enrolled at Kearney State College in Kearney, Nebraska, turning down a football opportunity at McCook Junior College. In September, America experienced the first-ever military

3

draft lottery broadcast live on TV. Tension filled the air as my friends and I watched birth dates scroll across the screen, knowing that the later a date appeared, the lower the likelihood of being drafted. That night determined the fate of every 18- to 26-year-old male in the nation. When my birth date finally flashed on the screen, it was number 264. I breathed a deep sigh of relief, realizing I probably wouldn't be called to serve. That moment set the trajectory of my life: I was never called to serve. However, many weren't as fortunate, and the national nightmare of the Vietnam War haunted the country for six more grueling years.

Chapter 2
I'm on my Way

Where am I goin'? I don't know.
When will I get there? I ain't certain.
All I know is I am on My Way.[1]

She was all girl, cute and fun. I met Cindy, the daughter of a farmer from a nearby town, during the summer of my junior year of college. For the next 18 months, we did the typical things that teenagers in love in rural areas do: go to movies, county fairs, dances, softball games in which I played, and attended an occasional concert. In the spring of 1972, I asked Cindy to marry me once I graduated from college.

In August of that year, I received my bachelor's degree in Business Administration from Kearney State College. A few weeks later, I drove to Colorado to look for a job. After a month of searching, I was offered a position with the Nabisco Company as a salesperson trainee. I eagerly accepted the offer and dashed back to Nebraska to prepare for our October wedding.

The morning after our wedding, the world seemed all new—one that was filled with endless possibilities. Neither of us really understood what it meant to be married, but we didn't care—we were young and in love.

We loaded as much stuff as the little Mustang would hold, pointed it west, and headed out for Cheyenne, Wyoming, where I was scheduled to work the following week. What a terrific final scene it would have made to a movie: driving into the sunset of the mountain west in our 1965 Mustang to live happily ever after. What an idyllic and naive dream. If only we knew.

Idyllic or not, the dream nearly came to a tragic ending ten days after our marriage. We had spent the first week in Cheyenne, Wyoming, where I filled in for a salesman who was on vacation. This was followed by a surrealistic, romantic weekend in

Yellowstone Park, where we had the entire park to ourselves; it had been officially closed for the season.

From there, we drove to Casper where I was scheduled to work the following week. As we prepared to leave for Denver the following Friday, word came that a massive snowstorm was building over the High Plains. However, with the bravery and foolishness of youth, I decided we were going anyway. For a while, all went well. However, just as nightfall began, we found ourselves in a blinding ground blizzard. As the wind whistled by at more than 30 mph, pellets of snow rocketed past the car like tiny ICBM missiles. I slowed the car to 10 mph with zero visibility to keep sight of the road. Twice, the car skidded into the median of the four-lane highway, but I gunned the motor enough to get the car back onto the tiny thread of blacktop. Finally, I opened the car door to keep sight of the middle line of the highway. I saw two tiny lights in the rearview mirror approaching us quickly. It was an 18-wheeler doing at least 50 mph. From his higher vantage point, the driver could see the road above the ground blizzard.

The mechanical monster's lights grew larger by the second as I tried to steer the car as far to the right as possible without running off the road. The glowing eyes bore down on us like a prehistoric creature preparing to pounce. Death seemed imminent. At the last moment, the lights disappeared from view, replaced by a gigantic wall of metal whooshing along the left side of the car, accompanied by a loud BOOM! BOOM! A split second later, the beast disappeared into a wall of swirling snow.

Shaken to our core, we crept along for another hour until we finally reached the safety of Cheyenne, Wyoming. Slowly opening the car door, I slid out and pulled my body upright. To my dismay, a wide black mark ran the entire length of the car. The rubber from the truck's tires screeched against our car as it roared past, barely missing us by half an inch. In that hair's breadth moment, I realized our lives must have a purpose; otherwise, God would have ended them right then and there.

Cindy and I loved our apartment in Arvada, Colorado. Although modest, it was our castle and a refuge from the world. Everything was exciting, and sometimes, as I sailed down I-29 for home after a long day at work, I sang the words to John Denver's "Rocky Mountain High" out loud. Life was fresh and new as I admired the rays from the setting sun splashing golden paint across dark green conifers, blanketing the front range of the Rockies. Those were happy days with Cindy cuddling beside me as we roared up into the mountains on weekends, exploring old mining towns, hiking, and seeking forgotten mountain roads leading to secret, magical places far from prying eyes.

But in spite of our happiness, the job was less than I had hoped for. I'd grown up stocking shelves in our grocery store and doing it again after going to college for four years didn't seem like much of a step up.

Nine months later, I resigned to enter the world of "high finance," or so I thought. After shamelessly lying on a personality test in order to "pass," I was hired by a finance company for $500 per month—even though I had no idea what a finance company was or what I would be doing. But I soon found out to my horror, I was a bill collector! Nothing could have been more of an affront to my shy personality!

As soon as I sat down at my little desk that first day, the manager plopped a pile of 3 by 5 cards in front of me and said, "Here, call these people about their medical bills." Stunned, I stared at the cards in silence. It was one of the most pivotal moments of my life. Should I do it or get up and walk out? After many minutes, I finally got the courage to pick up the phone and dial the number on the first card to collect a bill from some poor person who was down on their luck. It was the single hardest thing I had ever done at that point in my life, but it also proved to be pivotal to my future.

For the next nine months, I called people and went to their homes or places of employment to collect past-due loan payments, repossessed cars and motorcycles, and to "skip-trace" people who had moved without giving a forwarding address. It was a sleazy job run by sleazy people, one filled with some frightening experiences. I hated it!

In time, I became somewhat better as a bill collector. However, it's probably safe to say I was one of the worst at bill collecting the profession had ever seen. I was fired nine months later.

While losing the job was probably one of the best things that could have happened to me, it was still a major blow to my self-esteem. Quietly, I gathered my things and left the office for the last time and drove into the foothills of the Rockies as dusk turned to dark. Seeing a narrow canyon road, I turned in. Slowly, the car crept along, surrounded by canyon walls enveloped in the gloom. Finally, I pulled to the side of the road and let the car roll to a stop. There I sat, tears welling in my eyes but too proud to cry, the harsh realities of the world stinging my heart.

Suddenly, it felt as though someone else had entered the car. Then, in my mind, I heard, "Don't worry, everything is going to be fine." The words were calm and reassuring. Without knowing why, a sense of calm descended over me. Whoever or whatever came to me that night emanated a warm sense of love and compassion that I knew spoke the truth. It was the first but by no means the last time I would be assisted by angelic forces. With a restored sense of hope, I drove back to our new apartment in Lakewood.

Far from home without a job or a plan, I was in a quandary about what to do next. It was a critical juncture in our young lives, and I had no answers. Like a fighter staggered by a hard right to the head, the "real" world's calling card left me shaken and disillusioned.

The following week, I left for Nebraska. On a whim, I applied for a job with the Urban Renewal Authority in Grand Island. As with my previous job, I had no idea what the job entailed but the pay was more than I'd been making before, so why not? I filled out an application and had pretty much put the job out of my mind by the time I returned to Denver. A week later, I interviewed for the job and got it. My spontaneous decision to fill out a job application changed our lives forever.

I learned later that I got the job because they thought if I had the brazenness to be a bill collector, I probably had the moxie to do their job as well. How little they knew! It's funny how life works sometimes. Had I not been willing to take a chance to do something outside my comfort zone, new doors would never have opened for me.

Chapter 3
A Second Beginning

With the exuberance of youth, we returned to our roots in Nebraska and a second new beginning. My job with the Urban Renewal Authority in Grand Island, the third largest city in the state at 42,000, sounded exciting. The program had lofty goals of revitalizing poorer neighborhoods in a variety of ways for lower-income people. I was in charge of fixing up older homes. Although the program was controversial in conservative central Nebraska, I welcomed the opportunity to try to change the world for the better by making a positive impact in the community and on people's lives.

At first, I struggled to understand the ins and outs of renovating a home, but I grew into the position in time. As I was to discover at other times in my life, what at first appears to be complicated or insurmountable becomes old hat if you stick with it long enough. Over the next two years, we fixed nearly 100 homes.

While the program was a lightning rod of controversy, no one could deny we were making significant improvements to the community. By 1979, the program had increased the tax revenue in our redevelopment areas by 1000%.

Those early years in Grand Island were happy ones. After saving four years for a down payment, we bought a duplex. By living on one side and renting out the other, the extra income allowed us to save for a rainy day, even though we could never imagine there being one. Tennis after work, going to horse races, barbecuing at a nearby recreation area and taking trips were exciting and fun.

During this time of endless possibilities, something extraordinary occurred late one warm summer night. Around 3 a.m., I was suddenly startled awake, not knowing why. The only sound came from a few crickets chirping in the hope of a late-night rendezvous. Suddenly, the universe as I knew it began to change. My five senses began to merge as the cool night air mingled with the sound of the crickets, all of which radiated a warm sense of oneness. Within seconds, the feeling expanded until it encompassed the entire universe. It all happened so quickly that I couldn't comprehend what was happening. Suddenly, I was floating among the stars—or were they floating within me? They twinkled with an iridescence I'd never seen before and were intermingled with milky white galaxies of all shapes and sizes, some closer than others.

Everything was connected and I couldn't tell where I ended and the outside universe began. There was no space or time; everything was "one." I was part of the most distant galaxy and it was part of me. Then came a blizzard of energy all around me, coming, going, and just being. Stunned, the only coherent thought I could muster was, "Oh, my, what a busy place the universe is." Such feeble words give injustice to the majesty and grace of the universe I experienced that night. I'll never know how long the feeling lasted as there was no sense of time.

Finally, I drifted off to sleep. In the morning, still astounded, I vowed to recreate the intoxicating connectedness of the universe every day. Sadly, however, I never again fully experienced the sense of oneness that was revealed to me that magical summer night. It didn't matter. I knew I had been given a brief peek at the ultimate truth: that all things are connected. Mankind did not weave the web of life. We're merely strands in it and whatever we do to the web, we do to ourselves.

Things changed abruptly in July of 1979 when Sean was born. Our darling baby brought new meaning to our love, but little did we realize how much this little seven-pound bundle of joy was going to change our lives.

Ten days after Sean's birth, I received my Master of Business Administration degree from the University of Nebraska at Kearney. This was a huge accomplishment that represented the culmination of three and a half years of night classes and over a thousand miles of driving to other communities. The degree was more than a document to place on my office wall. It taught me not to listen to the judgments of others and to believe in myself.

In another ten days, my boss resigned. An hour later, I was named his replacement. Now called the Community Development Agency, I received a big raise. What a four-week period it had been!

While there still was a long way to go in the confidence department, I was beginning to see that hard work, belief in oneself, and the determination to stick with an idea took me farther in life than some of my old high school teachers ever thought possible.

These heady changes affected our lives in new and unexpected ways. While the baby gave life a new meaning, as with all babies, his needs took precedence over everything else. Our carefree life came to a screeching halt as "Baby Sean" controlled our every waking and (attempted) moments of sleep. I adapted to the new routine and so did Cindy; however, it affected her in ways I hadn't expected and could never fully understand. She became increasingly quiet and distant from me and finally sought counseling. She never shared the reason for her unhappiness with me. At one point, she asked if I would attend a counseling session with her? I refused. "Why?" I asked. "Nothing has changed between us." In retrospect, I should have been more involved in helping her overcome this crisis, regardless of the cause. It is something I have always regretted. Our relationship was never the same.

New job responsibilities were heaped on me, seemingly like cordwood. For the first time, I had to manage others, prepare budgets, speak publicly, deal with the media, lead or sit on committees, and deal with politicians. The task seemed daunting, but I put on a brave face and did the best to hide my inner doubts.

As I became more comfortable in my job, I developed various new programs and activities to stretch the money we received from the Housing & Urban Development (HUD) of the federal government. Before long, the Agency became known as an innovative and well-run program. But soon after that, disaster struck.

On June 3, 1980, seven tornadoes struck Grand Island and the surrounding area in what was the second-worst tornado disaster in the country's history up to that time. The storm system sat over the town for seven hours that night, spawning tornadoes. Meanwhile, our little family huddled in the basement of our house, not knowing if or when it was about to be torn to pieces. Fortunately, we weren't hit. My first waking memory on June 4th was the sound of a National Guard helicopter flying slowly over the house, the "whump, whump, whump" of its rotary blades reverberating in the air. All hell had broken loose. Three people were dead, hundreds injured, and over 150 square blocks of the city completely destroyed. The city was closed, and martial law was imposed. Armed National Guard troops patrolled everywhere.

President Carter declared Grand Island a National Disaster Area and personally inspected the devastation two weeks later. My life was turned upside down. Appointed grants coordinator, I was responsible for finding disaster relief funding for the city wherever possible. Our Agency was consumed with helping six neighborhoods of the city recover from the disaster for the next two years. A year after the tornadoes, everyone's hard work was acknowledged when the National Civic League declared Grand Island an "All-American City," and I was privileged to receive several awards and recognitions. A few years later, the Grand Island disaster was the subject of a popular book and Hollywood movie, both of which were named "The Night of the Twister."

What challenging but rewarding times those were! Life's circumstances were trying to force me out of the introverted shell that had been my safe haven for so many years. My boundaries were stretched in ways I never believed possible. I formed bonds with people from many different walks of life and saw the tremendous impact that caring for and working with one another can have in a time of crisis, or indeed, during any situation.

In early May 1983, Ryan was born. His fuzzy red hair was a dead giveaway of the German ancestry on his mother's side. He was a sweet baby who was reasonably well accepted by Sean as well as by our Boston Terrier, Duffy. We were now doubly blessed with two wonderful sons!

One morning, shortly after Ryan was born, something strange happened. As I got into the Mustang to go to work, I was surprised to see a walking cane laying across the front seat. I thought perhaps an old person, probably a man, had decided to sit inside the Mustang to admire the 1965 classic but forgot to take it with him when he left. But how could this be? The cane had obviously seen a lot of use and would have been important to the owner. I left the cane in the car for several days, expecting the owner to return to claim it. But no one ever did.

Perplexed, I shoved the cane into a closet. However, on Christmas Eve, I set it in the corner by the Christmas tree as a sign to the kids that Santa had come as in the movie "The Miracle of 34th Street." Eventually, we forgot about the mysterious cane. It would be many years before the significance of the cane was revealed.

They say life is a series of cycles. Too often it seems as though— just when things couldn't be better—the weather turns. Although no less dangerous than those that bear tornadoes, dark clouds of a different sort appeared on the horizon. In my case, the storm was brought on by people with a much different worldview than mine. While I had adapted well to my job responsibilities, I wasn't very good at the political game.

Grand Island was quite a conservative town, which was reflected in the mayor and two members of the city council. Although ours was a model program, before long these people were second-guessing our every decision. Their narrow and prejudicial way of viewing the world was upsetting to Cindy and me, but I was powerless to stop it.

Finally I had enough. Two months following Ryan's birth, in July 1983, I resigned from my position with the Community Development Agency. Sean was four years old at the time while little Ryan had only been with us for a few weeks.

I left the job with polarized emotions. I and others had made a real difference in the lives of many people, a majority of whom were minorities that had been forgotten or looked down upon by the rest of the people in town. Our program had rehabilitated over 60 dilapidated homes through grants and loan programs, purchased those beyond repair and relocated the families to nice ones of their choice with generous assistance, and upgraded the project area's infrastructure. As a result, we upgraded the area's tax base over 1000%.

Following the tornadoes on June 3, 1980, as grant coordinator for the City, I obtained and administered three programd that greatly assisted six devastated neighborhoods. These programs helped the courageous and determined people of Grand Island rebuild their community. A year later, Grand Island was designated an "All American City" by the National Civic League.

Personally, in 1980 I was honored by by the United States Junior Chamber of Commerce as one of the "Outstanding Young Men of America."
(https://en.wikipedia.org/wiki/Ten_Outstanding_Young_Americans)
I also received a "Housing Leadership" Award by the Nebraska Housing Group.

Finally, one of the programs we participated in with Lincoln and Omaha and the Nebraska Investment Finance Authority (NIFA), was recognized by HUD (Department of Housing of Urban Development) as one of the "Innovative Programs" in the nation.

My job as Director of the Community Development Agency was by far the most gratifying job I ever had or would hold.

While knowing it was a perilous gamble, my head was full of youthful idealism and—with eyes wide open—I led our little family straight into the abyss.

Chapter 4
New Directions

Ten years in the "School of Hard Knocks" had shown me the good, the bad, and the ugly of people in an up-close and personal way, shattering my idealistic perception of the world. It was a far different world than I had experienced with loving parents in the shelter of a small Nebraska town. However, although bruised and battered, I still believed that good and right would prevail in the long run.

Leaving the Community Development Agency in 1983 turned our world upside down. Gone was the steady income, health benefits and retirement program. Oblivious to these new realities, I busily went about setting up an office at home as an urban consultant and waiting expectedly for the phone to soon be ringing off the hook with new clients. What a rude awakening! Week after week went by as I sat at my desk waiting for the phone to ring in response to the many solicitations and advertisements I had sent. No one seemed interested. It was becoming evident that I knew nothing about marketing as an urban consultant. What in the world had I done?

Yet another week was dragging slowly by when, sitting alone in my office one afternoon, the phone rang. It was Tim, a friend from Lincoln who owned an urban consulting firm in Lincoln, Nebraska. "Mike," Tim said, "Becky and I are going to be making proposals to a number of communities that have been awarded urban redevelopment grants and wanted to know whether you would be interested in teaming up with us. Would I? In a heart-beat!

After agreeing to the details, we decided on a partnership, and before long, we were giving presentations to city councils or planning boards throughout the state. To Cindy's and my excitement, we landed jobs in two communities to develop redevelopment plans.

Being a consultant was exciting; however, more contracts were needed if the fledgling partnership was to survive. But fate intervened. Craig, the director of a state-funded Community Action Agency that provided limited technical assistance to small towns across the state, ignored the apparent conflict of interest and began utilizing established connections to city officials to snap up contracts that otherwise would have gone to private firms like ours. Business dried up fast and our little venture failed. Although Craig was to leave his job a few months later under a cloud of suspicion and investigation, the brief interconnection of our life paths altered mine forever. Funny, isn't it, how the timing of one seemingly small event can have such significant consequences in other areas?

But just as one door closed another opened. One day ut of the blue, I got a call from Jim, the owner of a local mortgage banking company. "Mike," he said, "Would you be interested in setting up a commercial loan department for my residential mortgage banking company? This really was "high finance" to me, but secretly I wondered whether I was up to the challenge. However, there was no going back. I was caught in the middle of a stream with a powerful current as life took me in exciting new directions whether I wanted to go along or not. In the past few months, the universe had manifested two completely unsolicited alternative possibilities for my career as well as our family's future. Somebody up there must like me, I reasoned airily, missing entirely the spiritual significance of what had taken place.

Working on a 100% commission basis, I dived into setting up the new loan department at the mortgage banker's home office in Grand Island. It was a huge undertaking and required personality skills that went entirely against the natural grain of my personality.

Little did I realize how out of my depth I was. Months of work, blending days into nights, saw me giving my all to succeed as a mortgage banker. But despite all my efforts, each deal unraveled for various reasons. Of course, no loans, no paycheck. The great sucking sound Cindy and I heard was our rapidly disappearing savings account.

One day, Jim called me into his office. "Mike," he said, "You're a nice guy who wants everyone to like you, but let's face it, you're just not cut out to be an income loan officer. I hate to see you

17

spending your money like this. Why don't you just give it up?" In silence, I stared back at him. He was calling me a failure, and it hurt inside. But the hurt soon turned to stubbornness and then anger. "No, I'm not giving up," I said.

"Ok," he shrugged. "It's your nickel." Had it not been "my nickel," I'm convinced he would have shown me the door and told me to use it.

More time rolled by as I struggled to carve out a niche in this elite, specialized profession. Fifteen months later, the financial end was near as only a few dollars remained in my twenty-three thousand dollars retirement account from the City of Grand Island. The time had come to accept defeat. But just as I was preparing to tell Jim things weren't going to work, the phone in my office rang. It was from a secondary market lender regarding an apartment application in another city that I sent him some time ago. "Mike, your loan on those apartments over in Kearney has been approved. We're sending you a commitment letter today." Ok, I answered feebly, not sure what else to say since--until then--I'd always failed. Afterward, with gallows humor, I rationalized that the only reason I succeeded must have been because I'd run out of ways to do things wrong.

My commission was $4,200, and it seemed like a million! The next day, an overdraft notice came from our bank. Our savings were wiped out! I smiled at the irony of the timing, coming one day after receiving my first paycheck in 15 months. Once again, just when things were at their darkest, the universe had provided. And, just as before, I didn't fully appreciate the irony of it all.

From that point onward, things in the loan business got easier. Had a greater power been testing me to see whether I was serious about pursuing my latest dream? Are we challenged in such ways? Or could it be that if you pursue a dream long enough, the dream will begin pursuing you?

As success mounted, I began to attract interest within the profession. In the fall of 1985, a headhunter representing a large mortgage banking company contacted me. We talked, and they offered me an excellent position with a prominent mortgage banker in Omaha that included an excellent salary and benefits package. After what I had been through the past two years, the offer was a dream come true. Still, there was much to consider. Cindy and I talked about it far into the night. After considering everything, we decided it was an opportunity I couldn't refuse, so I accepted the job offer.

I gave notice. But suddenly, my employer had a new-found interest in me. The company that had let me twist in the wind for 15 months and told me I didn't have the mettle for the job suddenly pleaded for me to stay. "Mike," Jim said, "You've worked so hard to make this thing go. I hate seeing you give it all up just as you're on the verge of making big money in this business. Stay with us. Pick where you want to go, Omaha or Kansas City. We'll match their salary, give you 50% of all commissions, a company car, and an expense account."

While skeptical of my employer's newly found interest in my well-being, there were many things to consider. This could be my one opportunity to "go for the gold," as they say, and become the head of an entire commercial mortgage banking network-- with all the benefits and privileges such a position entails. So, after talking things over with Cindy, we decided I should stay with my current employer but move to Kansas City.

As awkward and uncomfortable as it was to do so, I withdrew my acceptance of the offer from the large mortgage banking company, and we began making arrangements to move to Kansas City. It was a long throw of the dice and I've always wonder whether it was the right decision.

Chapter 5
Goin' to Kansas City

Cindy and I decided it would be best if I moved first to find a place for us to live, so in January 1986, I loaded the Mustang, kissed Cindy and the boy's goodbye, and left for Kansas City with Duffy at my side. It was both a sad and happy moment in our lives. But once again, things were on the upswing.

I rented a house in Olathe, Kansas, a suburb of Kansas City. When school was out in May, we rented and loaded up a U-Haul and for the last time left our home in Grand Island for the past ten years. Sean and Ryan were excited to have a new house and yard to explore. I assumed Cindy felt the same way, and so it seemed for a while. However, after a while it became obvious she was not happy. Little things grew into shouting matches. On more than one occasion, she screamed, "Why did you drag me and the boys down here?"

I was confused. She never explained why she resented the move so strongly or why she hadn't expressed these feelings until after the move. We had mutually agreed to move to Kansas City.

While we had some good times, usually revolving around Sean and Ryan, it became clear that we simply had different views and objectives regarding many things in life. The distance between us slowly grew more expansive over time.

Initially the job went well and the perks of the position were nice. However, before there was enough time to get the Commercial Loan Department fully operational, my employer—the same one who had begged me to stay with them so we could build a strong financial future together—sold the company to a firm out of Detroit that didn't plan to continue the commercial division. Following a handshake, two weeks' severance pay and no apologies, I was left unemployed. While owners Jim and Steve enjoyed their golden parachutes, I was stiffed for the second time in less than a year. So much for trust and loyalty.

In January, I began what I feared would be an arduous search for a new job. To my surprise, two weeks later, I got an offer from a mortgage company out of Oklahoma City to be their commercial loan office's vice president and branch manager. The financial terms were acceptable and I went to work hoping that perhaps this time I'd find a stable employer. No such luck. Six months later, the company declared bankruptcy amid rumors of financial scandal and drug use by one of the owners. Once again, I was out on the street.

Cindy was rightfully angry over this latest job fiasco, as well as for the entire trauma I'd put her and the family through the past four years since leaving my job with the Community Development Agency.

It would have been so easy to be bitter on life. Of course I was acrimonious, but I still believed the hard times were just bumps in the road and that the future would be bright if we worked through them.

I scanned the paper for months and contacted private employment agencies without luck. The good news was that I finally had more time to be with Sean and Ryan. I cherished taking Sean, who was seven years old by now, to swimming lessons and playing with four-year-old Ryan. These were priceless times in a child's life and I relished our times together.

Finally, in early 1988, I was offered a job as Vice President and head of the loan department for a five-hundred-million-dollar local savings and loan association. In December of that year, more good fortune came our way when, after nearly two years of looking, we found our dream home just a block from where we'd been renting. We moved into the new house shortly after Christmas. Magic filled the air!

The following two years were busy but finally content. Cindy and I worked hard to make a good life for our sons and spent every possible moment with them. At ages ten and six, Sean and Ryan were within the golden ages that parents love. Perhaps most importantly, Cindy finally resolved herself to living in Kansas City, and things got better between us.

While I thrived on the fast pace and responsibilities of a corporate officer position at the S&L, I was expected to join an exclusive country club, a requirement I found incompatible with my values. And try as I might, some of the beliefs and values of upper management and their social set simply went against the grain of how I was raised. It had taken me 15 years to realize my dream of a career in "high finance," only to realize that its world contradicted who I was and what I believed.

In January of 1990, a friend told me about the Resolution Trust Corporation (RTC), which had been created to clean up a crisis in the savings and loan industry. It was one of the worst economic disasters in the country's history and would ultimately cost taxpayers billions of dollars. While the RTC was only designed to exist for five years, it offered a wealth of career opportunities and high salaries. I interviewed and was offered a job as an Asset Manager. The offer was too good to pass up so, in February of 1990, I joined the Kansas City office of the RTC.

This time, my decision proved to be the right move as a year later RTC took over the S&L where I'd worked. It joined the ranks of hundreds of other institutions that were sold or dissolved by RTC. Within eighteen months, I was promoted to Senior Environmental Program Manager for the 50 billion-dollar asset office.

The scope of the job proliferated. Before long, I was managing a staff of thirteen people. Too often I worked late into the night before going home, at last stumbling through the door and collapsing into the nearest easy chair, too tired to play with the boys or talk to Cindy.

Despite a busy schedule, I prepared for life after RTC. It was essential because the organization was scheduled to go out of existence in 1995. So in 1993, I began taking classes in real estate appraising as a way to expand my job skills. Two years later, I passed the state test for residential and commercial property appraisers.

In 1995, the Kansas City office of the Resolution Trust closed and 250 employees scrambled to find new jobs. Twelve lucky people, including me, were offered 12-month assignments in Chicago with the Federal Deposit Insurance Corporation (FDIC) to help finish RTC's work. Although the position was temporary, the pay was far more than I'd ever earned and there was the possibility I would be offered a full-time position with the federal government.

Job prospects in Kansas City were dismal at the time. Although the thought of being away from Sean and Ryan for the better part of a year sickened me, after talking it over with Cindy, we decided it was a chance worth taking. So in May 1995, Sean and Ryan accompanied me to Lisle (a southwest suburb of Chicago), where I had rented a studio apartment, and stayed a few days.

At the end of their visit, I silently watched their plane lift into the sky above Midway Airport headed for Kansas City. Tears filled my eyes. Even though we believed the decision was in the family's best interests, somehow it felt wrong. I walked slowly to my car, started the motor, and drove away to begin yet another new chapter in our lives.

Chapter 6
The Awakening

After living in a house full of dogs, cats, and kids, my little studio apartment in Lisle was quite a shock to the system. Even though Kansas City was a large city, especially for someone from a town of about 700 in Nebraska, it couldn't hold a candle to the overwhelming size of the Chicago metroplex. I became another faceless commuter whose life was dictated by the city. Each day followed a long, monotonous schedule. However, by working an extra hour each day I was off every other Friday, which allowed me to return to Kansas City and spend a short weekend with my family.

The good news was that the long daily train and bus commute to and from the city afforded me an unexpected amount of free time. One day on the way to the train station, I passed a bookstore. On a whim, I stepped inside looking for something to read during my commutes. Casually browsing the long stacks of books, engulfed by the slightly musky aroma and sense of tranquility bookstores provide, I came to the science and spirituality section. All the titles sounded fascinating, but one caught my eye: *Physics and Philosophy*.[1] I bought it.

I had always been spiritual but rarely attended church, except for the Unitarian Church a few years earlier, mainly to give Sean and Ryan some religious guidance. As a child of the rebellious sixties, I felt organized religion was mostly judgmental and hypocritical. Instead, I learned more from my mother's wisdom with whom I had long conversations on such topics as "Who is God?" and "What is the meaning of life and the universe?" I had two wonderful, loving parents, but Mom was exceptional. Intelligent and deeply compassionate toward all living things, she introduced me to Christian Science. It espoused that each of us is capable of healing ourselves through the power of the mind.

Thus began a period of intense curiosity. The long train ride to and from the city became a precious opportunity to devour books regarding the "how and why" of the universe. Slowly, the mind-boggling world of quantum mechanics began to reveal itself to me. Around this time, I became friends with Lona, a co-worker, and her husband, Wendell. The three of us talked far into the night regarding the meaning of life.

My new friends introduced me to the "Association of Research and Enlightenment" (ARE), founded on the teachings of Edgar Cayce, "The Sleeping Prophet." Cayce gave thousands of readings to individuals while in a trance-like state over a period of 30 years in the early 20th century. The information from Cayce dealt with many topics, including health, medical cures and earth changes, many of which were astoundingly accurate. Fascinated, I attended meetings on topics such as psychic abilities, the paranormal, prophecies, and the nature of God. My head swam with new ideas and possibilities. It was the beginning of a journey that was to have no end, and little did I realize how important this knowledge would become in the coming years.

While my exposure to novel ideas in Chicago was exhilarating, I greatly missed my family. In addition, the financial burden of maintaining two households and the travel costs between Chicago and Olathe quickly took their toll. More importantly, raising newly minted teenager Sean became a real strain for Cindy without a father's hand. Because of this, I regretted taking the job in Chicago. On the other hand, the move started me on an important spiritual journey that otherwise may not have happened. And had that journey not taken place, my future might have been drastically different. Could it be true that everything happens for a reason?

Ten months later, the dreams of all 12 of us Kansas City transplants to land permanent jobs with the federal government came crashing down. All of us from Kansas City were to be let go at the end of May 1996. Once again, I faced the unknown after a job gamble came up empty-handed. This was becoming an increasingly common occurrence!

What am I going to do this time, I thought. Should I return to real estate, the profession I knew best, or continue the environmental career path of the past five years? Night after night, I lay awake staring at the ceiling, pondering the best way to allow our family to remain in Kansas City. It was yet another critical fork in the road.

One day, I ran into my friend Lona in the lunchroom and shared my dilemma with her. "Have you ever heard of a Novena prayer,"[2] she asked. I had not. "Say the prayer every day for two weeks, starting with 14 times the first day and one less each succeeding day, and that for which you pray will come true," she said. At first, I scoffed at the idea but then decided, oh well, why not give it a try? I have nothing to lose.

But before I could begin saying the Novena, I needed to determine my heartfelt desire. This wasn't as easy as it first appeared. What do I really want in life: a big salary, an important job with a lot of responsibility, a fancy office with a personal secretary? What would you wish for?

Finally, after days of pondering, an answer popped into my head: "Happiness." More specifically, happiness in Kansas City. That's it! After all, what is more important than happiness?

For the next two weeks, every day I recited the words to the Novena prayer, inserting my new and strong desire for "happiness in Kansas City" where appropriate. I recited and repeated the prayer while waiting for the train, riding to or from work, on the bus back to the apartment, and while jogging. The prayer, I learned later, is called the "Infant Jesus Novena" and is often said in cases of urgency. It goes as follows:

Jesus said, "Ask and You shall receive, seek and you shall find, knock and the door shall be opened to you."

Through the intercession of Mary, Thy Most Holy Mother, I knock, I seek and I ask that my prayer be granted.

(Make your request.)[3]

While the influence of the prayer on what happened can be debated, the fact was that within three weeks I received two job offers in the Kansas City area. One was as a market representative with an environmental investigation company, while the other was an appraiser with a commercial real estate appraisal company.

Would the job offers have come my way without the Novena prayer? I'll let the readers decide. I just considered it another example of "like attracting like." Ever notice how people with positive attitudes seem to have good things come their way? Likewise, people with negative or grumpy attitudes often seem to have negative things happen to them. I had seen both situations occur so often by now that it had to be more than a coincidence. I had read about the secret behind how this principle works.

To successfully manifest your desires, it is essential to set a clear goal and consistently maintain a focused state of mind. Merely wishing for something and quickly shifting attention to another desire is insufficient. Continuously put energy, thought, feeling, and voice into your unfulfilled desires as though they've already happened.

The longer this is done, the more we will attract the things we desire. Perhaps that's why the Novena is supposed to be repeated daily for two weeks.

In the words of Mahatma Gandhi:

Your beliefs become your thoughts

Your thoughts become your words

Your words become your actions

Your actions become your habits

Your habits become your values

Your values become your destiny.[4]

After mulling over the alternatives, I decided to follow a lesson learned years ago: put aside ego and accept the opportunity that presented the best long-term possibilities regardless of salary in the short run. I decided to return to the field of real estate and become an appraiser even though it would be the hardest occupation to thoroughly learn, all the while receiving a paltry salary that was on a commission-only basis. In early June 1996, I said goodbye to Chicago and went home to Kansas City.

Chapter 7
Home Again

It was great to be back with the family full-time. Seeing how much the boys had grown in the past year made me realize how much precious time I had missed with them while they were still kids. It cut deep. Trying to make up for lost time, I spent as much time with them as possible, including taking the family on a memorable trip to New Orleans and rural Louisiana. But while our lives quickly became entwined again, something important had been lost. Both of my sons were now at the stage of life when the bonds between parent and child were subtly yet steadily loosening. While this drifting is a natural and integral part of every young person's journey from childhood to becoming an adult, I felt helpless watching those fleeting golden times disappear like sand through an hourglass.

To make things worse, I was knee-deep in trying to learn how to appraise commercial properties. In one of the hardest things I'd ever done, night after night, my light was the only one in the office as I struggled to figure things out.

Finally, long past the due date, I turned in my first appraisal and nearly collapsed with relief when I returned to my desk. The work was marginal at best, but it was a start. There had to be better days ahead—or so I told myself. Over the next 18 months, appraising became easier as I gained experience, but it was always a struggle as there was something new in every assignment. The pay was so poor that finally, without telling my employer, I took a part-time job working nights for a collection agency to earn some extra cash to help pay the bills. The hated duties were a step back in time to my disastrous foray as a bill collector in Colorado, but, once again, it served its purpose. By now, our family's fortunes had been up and down so many times that I had almost lost count.

The ebb and flow reminded me of the words to Frank Sinatra's "That's Life," part of which goes as follows:

I've been a puppet, a pauper, a pirate, a poet, a pawn, and a king.

I've been up and down and over and out,

And I know one thing:

Each time I find myself flat on my face,

I pick myself up and get back in the race.[1]

I resumed mentoring young people and was honored as "Youth Friend of the Year" by the Olathe Schools District. Concurrently, Mahaffie School, where I'd been mentoring, gave me an "Inspiration" award.

The words seemed prophetic. I plunged ahead, two steps forward, one step back, for the sake of those I loved. Once again, it was Cindy's steady work and stable income that helped keep the family afloat financially during times of difficulty. Even though we had personal differences, we were fighters united behind one cause: ensuring Sean and Ryan's well-being.

During these times, the fascinating world of quantum mechanics often dominated my thoughts. The topic was confusing, to put it mildly, but somehow it seemed important to try to understand. Slowly, ever so slightly, an entirely new level of reality was revealed:

- An object can be in many places at the same time.
- If two subatomic particles within an atom are separated by miles, and the spin of one particle is changed, the other will also change instantaneously—faster than the speed of light.
- The entire universe is made up of vibrations of information-filled energy that can exist both as a visible particle and an invisible wave. Incredibly, they only change from a wave to a particle if they're observed, and sometimes, the observer's intention determines the type of particle that takes shape.
- Quantum particles communicate with themselves at different points in time. In other words, they are not limited by our understanding of the past, present, and future.

- To a quantum particle, "then is now, and there is here."[2,3,4]

The implications were mind-blowing! Everything is connected and space and time don't exist at the quantum level. Even more impressive was the fact that we directly affect the manifestation of innumerable types of particles in the universe. In short, the universe responds to our beliefs. I read about John Wheeler, an honored Princeton physicist and colleague of Einstein, who once said we live in a "participatory universe" in which consciousness plays a vital and necessary role.[5] The more I was able to grasp these ideas, the more elegant, beautiful, and miraculous the universe became.

The revelations of the quantum universe caused me to reconsider some long-held beliefs and skepticism regarding organized religion. Even though I believed all religions based on love are correct at the faith level, I had trouble getting past the judgment, condemnation, and fear-based teachings that some denominations seem to espouse. Then I remembered Unity Church, which my friend Lona had once told me about.

Promising myself I'd only go once to check it out, the following Sunday, I quietly slipped into the back pew of the sanctuary at Unity Church of Overland Park, ready to bolt at the first sound of any of the "red flag" code words I'd come to know so well. The words never came. Instead, I kept hearing about the importance of such things as love and non-judgment. Intrigued, I went a second time, then a third. I was becoming hooked but disappointed when Cindy wasn't interested in joining me.

On the work front, one month blended into the next. The job had only limited income potential but still required many hours and years of experience to fully master. It was a situation I could not accept. So when I heard of an opening with a large bank as a commercial review appraiser, I applied. However, with no response I eventually forgot about the position.

None too soon, the long winter finally released its grip, while signs of spring began popping up here and there. While driving back to the office one afternoon, I noticed a grotto by a Catholic church in honor of Our Lady of Lourdes. On a whim, I pulled the car to the curb and shut off the engine. The grotto reminded me of one I had discovered while living in Chicago. One in which I cherished the solitude, connectedness with nature, and spiritual energy that it pervaded. Reverently walking over to the shrine, I discovered a small stone bench in front of a man-made enclave. The flickering light from several prayer candles inside the enclave gave a comforting glow. Sitting on the bench admiring the beauty of the rock enclosure, I became one with my surroundings as the here and now dissipated. Eventually, the failing job situation came to mind while I quietly whispered a prayer for guidance. More minutes passed when suddenly a message popped into my mind from "somewhere": You will have a good job by the end of the year. Intuition? Divine revelation? Whatever it was, the thought gave me sorely needed comfort.

The endless rhythm of the seasons continued as spring turned into summer. Once again, Little League baseball dominated our lives. Cindy and I spent many summer evenings watching seemingly endless baseball games in which Sean and Ryan played. Other times, we barbecued in the backyard, our cares temporarily forgotten.

As the leaves turned crimson following crisp autumn evenings, life's routine was unexpectedly shaken one Friday when I received a call from the bank to which I had applied for a job many months earlier. The next day, I found myself sitting in a coffee shop at Kansas City International Airport, talking to a senior executive for its Midwest Region. The following Monday, I was offered a job with a good salary and attractive benefits. I gladly accepted.

This latest position was everything I had dreamed of but somehow not too surprising. For months, there'd been the sense that something good was going to happen. Had the grotto's message been a portent that the Novena prayer for happiness in Kansas City would soon be realized? Or was it just another one of life's coincidences? Only time would tell, but my expectations reminded me of something 19th-century psychologist and philosopher William James once said: "If you want quality [in life], act as if you already have it. If you want a trait, act as if you already have the trait."[6] In other words, what we believe and expect to happen in our daily lives has a direct and consequential effect on what actually happens.

With less financial stress and more free time, I put into practice some of the ideals I'd learned from my new spiritual awareness: be more open and understanding, appreciate the moment, be less driven by material success, and give more of your time to others. I became a mentor with the "Youth Friends" program as a "lunch buddy" for several boys, aged 5 to 7, who were having trouble coping with some things in their lives. The setting created the safe, supportive, non-threatening environment they desperately needed. I mentored several boys for the next six years, including five years with a highly intelligent and complex boy named Jared.

By now, 17-year-old Sean was a junior in high school. His hard work paid off and he became a starting offensive lineman on his state championship-winning football team. Cindy, Ryan, and I enjoyed watching him and his team play football on crisp Friday evenings throughout the fall. Ryan was in the eighth grade and played Pony League baseball every year until age 18. He was a good hitter, and we spent many long, warm summer evenings watching his heroics. Cindy and I knew those golden days with our sons would pass all too quickly. I wondered what life would be like without them.

In the years since Sean's birth, Cindy's personality changed as the difficulties of motherhood set in. However, I don't think I fully realized her unhappiness until I came across an essay on her desk entitled "Running Away" that she'd written for a psychology class she was taking. In it, she lamented the drudgery of her life as a wife and mother and expressed how desperately she wanted to run away to escape it all. She didn't, she wrote, because of little things, such as when one of the boys brought her a dandelion as a present.

Each day after work, we talked about the day's events and only rarely had arguments. From my perspective, things seemed to be going smoothly even though after expressing my opinion on a subject I was passionate about, Cindy's response was either silence or an obligatory "that's nice." Nevertheless, I naively assumed we agreed on most topics and often acted on those assumptions.

However, her unexpected rants of "Everything always has to be done your way!" should have been a clear warning sign. Not knowing where she stood on an issue left me confused, frustrated, and unsure of myself. From the first days of our marriage, I had tried to arouse in her the same ambitions and curiosity about the world that I felt. I'm sure she tried; however, not surprisingly, she couldn't change the person she was. The simple truth was that we had vastly different goals, ambitions, and views of the world that were magnified with each passing year. Why didn't we heed those warning signs? It's a question unanswered.

Aside from our commitment to the boys, we shared an interest in antiques and enjoyed traveling to see anything of a historical nature. Beyond that, our interests in life diverged. She enjoyed reading romance or science fiction novels, painting landscape pictures, designing Fabergé eggs, and doing things with Judy, the mother of one of Ryan's Little League teammates. I enjoyed attending classes or reading about topics involving science and spirituality, being active in politics and genealogy, and doing outdoor things such as hiking and bicycling.

Different ideas on how to raise children also widened the schism. While not a strict disciplinarian or someone who held high expectations concerning work, I did expect the kids to do their share, as had been expected of me when I was that age. On the other hand, Cindy seemed to relish playing the role of "good cop" to ingratiate herself with them; not a healthy situation for any of us.

Chapter 8
Longs Peak

As I sat absently staring out the open patio door from my couch onto our tree-filled yard, a Colorado mountain came to mind on a breezy spring day in 1998. Oh, how I used to dream of climbing it! Longs Peak is located near Estes Park, Colorado, and has been called the "monarch of the North Front Range" of the Rockies because it towers above all the other mountains. My brother and I used to talk for hours about climbing the mountain together, but life got in the way. We both had moved back to Nebraska in the early 1970s and, 15 years later, Rod had a severe heart attack. Although he recovered, Rod's mountain climbing dreams were over. Meanwhile, I'd gotten overweight and out of shape. The objective of climbing Longs Peak seemed dead.

Just for kicks, I researched the Internet. Longs Peak is 15th among Colorado's 52 peaks over 14,000 feet and is considered one of the outstanding peaks in North America. The most popular "non-technical" route (i.e., ropes not used) is called "The Keyhole," a 16-mile round trip with 4,850 feet of vertical ascent and several precipitous drop-offs. Over 10,000 people try to climb the mountain each year, but only half succeed. And last but not least, over 80 people have been killed climbing the mountain.[1]

The obstacles were numerous.

- I was too old.
- I was too fat and out of shape.
- I'd never climbed a mountain before
- I'd have to go alone. (Cindy didn't like hiking, little less
- mountain climbing.)
- The mountain was dangerous and deadly. Roughly 80 people have died trying to climb it over the years.

What a silly and impossible idea. In fact, it bordered upon madness! Or did it? Carefully, I searched for an answer to each obstacle:

- Too old? I'm only 49. That may be old in some people's eyes, but I certainly don't feel old.
- Fat and out of shape? What better reason to get into shape?
- Never climbed a mountain before? Educate yourself about the secrets to successful high-country hiking. Become very familiar with the specific dangers of the mountain.[2]
- No one to go with? Then go alone.
- Too hard? The only limitations we have are those that we place upon ourselves.
- Too dangerous? Be extra careful and cautious.

Slowly, I mulled each idea over in my mind. It still seemed like a crazy idea, but I was bored with my suddenly easy life. A goal, however improbable, was what I needed. Besides, if the goal proved to be too difficult, all I needed to do was turn around and go back down.

Longs Peak

Everyone thought my idea was nuts! But I wouldn't be deterred. If nothing else, it would motivate me to get back into shape. So in the spring of 1998, I began working out for the first time in years. After the first day, every muscle in my body seemed to scream in unison: "What are you doing to me? Why are we not vegging out while watching TV and eating potato chips?" The second day was worse, and the third was worse than the first. But the pain and

35

stiffness had considerably subsided when I got up on the morning of the fourth day. From that point, my workouts became easier and easier. It felt good to be physically active again after so many years, and as my physical condition improved, I began losing weight and feeling better. By July, I was walking or running four to five miles a night, and my dream became stronger. The dream didn't seem quite as unbelievable as before.

However, two weeks before I planned to leave, Cindy shocked me by saying she wouldn't come. She didn't give a reason. Could it have been spite? I'll never know. Regardless, I was devastated. Had it not been for Dad, I wouldn't have gone.

After making reservations the first week in August at a motel in Estes Park, Colorado, near Longs Peak in Rocky Mountain National Park, I picked up Dad in Nelson and we made the seven hour drive to the beautiful Rocky Mountains. However, the event was marred from the beginning by a series of roadblocks:

On the morning of the climb, rain forced me to cancel. So we drove over the breathtaking Trail Ridge Road and checked into a cabin outside of Grand Lake. However, proving Dad was right that I was stubborn as a Missouri Mule, two days later I got up at midnight and began the dangerous drive back over Trail Ridge Road in the fog. It was white-knuckle all the way, and I narrowly missed an Elk standing in the middle of the road. I hit the trail head around 1:30 a.m. and away I went. But alas, I was forced to turn around at 13,000 feet because of extremely dangerous black ice. Even after turning back, I slipped and fell 10 feet onto a boulder, dislocating a finger. Lucky I didn't break a leg.

Although the trip was ill-fated from the start, I had accomplished more than what seemed possible sitting in my easy chair a year earlier. And in the trying, I discovered something even more important: **I'm not a helpless victim to the whims of life with no recourse but to watch myself grow older, year after year, awaiting the death's inevitability. No! I'm in control, and the only things holding me back are the self-created doubt and limitations of my imagination. The world is filled with**

possibilities! And as an added bonus, Dad and I shared precious moments together that lasted a life-time.

Long's Peak 1999
The Second Attempt

Back in the "real" world of day-to-day living, the following year—1999—was vital for us as Sean graduated from high school. But our happiness was bittersweet because we knew he'd be leaving to attend the University of Kansas in just a few short months.

That spring, I decided to try to climb Longs Peak one more time. But this time, armed with valuable experience, I did things differently. I trained earlier, harder, and carefully outlined a strategy to ensure success.

To my surprise, Cindy agreed to come along. While delighted, it was indicative of the unpredictability of our relationship. We left for Colorado the first week of August. Following two successful practice climbs, we spent a day enjoying the bucolic beauty in and around Estes Park. On the day before the climb, talking more than we had in years, I was reminded of why we got together in the first place. Whether it was because we didn't have the stress of jobs, kids for a change, or something else, I wondered why things couldn't always be like this. I still wonder.

Our enjoyment was dampened the day before the climb when a climber fell 500 feet to his death at the 13,000-foot level, the third person to die on or near Longs Peak in the last ten days. For one of the few times in my life, the hair on the back of my neck raised.

We returned to the motel in silence. In spite of the recent bad karma on the mountain, I left the motel at 1:00 a.m. the next morning, exactly as planned. I signed the registration box at the trailhead, took a deep breath, and strode into the darkness. My boots crunching the rocks on the trail broke the utter silence. It was a surrealistic world of silently watching spruce and pine silhouettes with ghostly arms reaching down toward the slender path snaking through the forest. Was I the only living creature in this eerie domain? The tiny beam from my headlamp feebly pierced the pervasive blackness of the forest, making a narrow gash of less than ten feet of the trail in front of me. Relentlessly, the route took me higher and higher. After some hours of walking, the trees became increasingly smaller and the terrain more barren until there were no trees. This was tree line and the Arctic Tundra region, where there isn't enough oxygen to support trees and many kinds of life.

As I trudged along the trail, life was simple—no worries about my job, retirement plan, or the state of the union. No regretting the past or worrying about the future. All that mattered was the small section of trail directly in front of me illuminated by my headlamp. I also thought of my brother. Life had dealt him a hand that ended his dream of accomplishing many physical goals, so he couldn't be with me. The climb was for both of us.

Right foot forward, crunch, tap, left foot forward, crunch, tap—on and on I went upward. The cool early morning air was heavy with dew and felt refreshing on my sweat-beaded brow. The deep forest was as silent as a tomb, broken only by the sounds of my feet crunching rocks on the trail, the tapping of my walking sticks and the creaking of my daypack. As the minutes turned into hours, I became aware of something I'd always known but had forgotten: the only thing that really matters in life is the present moment. It is the only thing over which we have complete control.

After three hours or so, it was time for a break. With a grunt, I lifted the pack from my back and let it drop with a thud. Then it happened: lifting my head to drink from my canteen, my eyes saw something they had never seen before. The sky was filled with diamonds the size of peas. No matter where I looked, precious gems glistened and sparkled, winking at me as though alive. Transfixed, time stood still as I gazed up at the magnificent cosmos. Then it hit me. I had lived my entire life without realizing that such a world existed. How foolish to have wasted most of my life worrying about frivolities while missing what truly mattered: the miracle and indescribable beauty of the living universe around us, one in which we are privileged to participate. In that spectacular moment, my perception of life was forever changed.

Four hours later, the Boulder Field came into view, dwarfed by the outline of the "Diamond," a 1,200-foot sheer wall of rock that was the mighty face of Longs Peak. Following a brief rest, I switched from my cumbersome daypack to a smaller fanny pack, knowing the most challenging part of the day was about to begin, including steep inclines filled with large boulders and dangerous gaps in between and 1,000 to 2,500-foot drop-offs from a poorly marked trail.

Sometime later, picking my way carefully along the trail, a curious scene came into view. An overweight man in his late 20s was sitting on a rock crying as an older man leaned close to him, whispering. As I passed, I heard the overweight fellow say, "I'm scared. I've never been this high before. I can't do it." "Yes, you can," the other man said, "Don't give up now." Before going around a corner, I glanced back and saw the young man slowly pulling himself to his feet.

Many more challenges lay ahead that morning. At times, my leg quivered with fatigue and anxiety. I scarcely noticed the incredible beauty of a precipitous thousand-foot drop to a dark green forested valley, many thousands of feet below, through which flowed a tiny ribbon of deep blue water that probably was a decent-sized mountain stream.

Eventually, the trail came to a dead end before a wall of boulders in front and left, with a precipitous thousand-foot drop-off on the right. This was the "Loft," a 900-foot rock wall at a 50-60 percent incline. Taking a deep breath, I gazed at the mighty wall and whispered softly, "Well, Dorothy, we're not in Kansas anymore." Finding a handhold on the nearest boulder, I pulled upward. One down and about a million to go, I thought. Slowly making my way up the long rubble of boulders one handhold at a time, the only sounds were my breath and beating heart. One slip could be fatal.

After what seemed forever, I came to a small, flat terrace. What a relief to finally stand on level ground! However, the worst was yet to come: a 10-foot vertical wall. It was one of the mountain's sternest tests to determine who was worthy of conquering it. Had I been with a companion, it would have been relatively easy to surmount but doing it alone was an entirely different matter. Repeatedly, I jumped as high as possible, trying to catch a handhold. Each time I failed, plunking back onto the small platform dangerously close to the precipice. Finally, gasping in the thin air, I saw a small crack near the top. With defeat staring me in the face, I gathered my strength for one final try. To my surprise, I felt the tiny crevice in my hand and tightened my grip around it. Holding on for dear life, I pulled, clawed, kicked, and wriggled my way to the top. Once there, I flopped onto my back, gasping for air, staring into an impossibly blue sky.

Now came "The Narrows," a 50-foot-long section of trail about 18 inches wide with a rock wall on one side but a sheer 900-foot drop-off on the other. A large rectangular boulder at the bottom was aptly named "The Hearse." Inching along the tiny path, I remembered reading nightmarish stories about climbers caught in "The Narrows" during violent thunderstorms with high wind, pelting rain, and lightning that electrified the rock wall against which they were clinging. "Thank God, there's good weather today," I whispered. After a few minutes, but what seemed like hours, "The Narrows" ended.

The final obstacle was the "Homestretch," a 300-foot incline filled with sharp-angled boulders. Ignoring my weary legs, I stepped onto a boulder, reaching for yet another handhold. The end was near—nothing could stop me now. As I progressed, the best holds kept moving me to the right until eventually, I was up against a rock wall. The only way to go was up. Near the top, I snuck a peek over the edge of the rock face to see—"nothing." Nothing but sky and hazy blue peaks far, far into the distance. Thousands of feet below me, looking like a tiny puddle, was Bear Lake, a popular tourist destination. Too intimidated to enjoy the view, I quickly looked away.

A few minutes later, at about 9:00 in the morning, I pulled myself over a ledge and plopped onto flat ground, gasping for oxygen in the thin mountain air. Several minutes later, I pulled myself upright using a walking stick to gaze upon a level boulder-strewn area about 300 feet in diameter. This was it: the summit.

Mountains stretched to the horizon on all sides. To the east were the High Plains of eastern Colorado, stretching across 200 miles to the Nebraska border. To the north lay the "Never Summer" and "Mummy" Ranges. The mountains of Wyoming could be seen, tiny blue jagged lines far to the north. Mountain peaks were to the west and south until finally disappearing into the mist. I had become one of only 2 percent of people on Earth to stand more than 14,000 feet above sea level.

Drinking in the beauty and significance of the moment, I never felt more alive. When I signed the register placed there by the Park Service, I wrote "Touch the Face of God" in the present rather than past tense because I wanted to remind people that they could experience the Divine in every moment of their lives—not only at surreal places such as mountaintops.

My magical moment at the second-highest place in the continental United States was cut short 15 minutes later when I noticed a rain shower several miles to the northwest. A light blue curtain of rain wafted from the cloud to Earth below. It was moving in my direction. While mesmerizing, rain, lightning, and slippery wet rocks were not on the day's itinerary. So with a sigh of regret, I began the descent with a young climber from Seattle. While it's well known that going down is the most dangerous part of a mountain climb, mine was mostly uneventful except for one crucial event. As I was maneuvering my way back down the arduous loft, I met the overweight man I'd seen earlier who wanted to turn around. He and his friend were working their way up the loft. But this time, he didn't look distraught. His sweaty face was filled with determination. With a big smile, I gave him two thumbs up. Great job, I said, you're almost there! He smiled but didn't say a word. Undoubtedly he succeeded in reaching the summit by facing his fear and conquering it.

The trip down was filled with beauty, wonder and awe as nature put on a spectacular once-in-a-lifetime display for my benefit. Cumulous clouds appeared out of thin air yards from the trail. Heated by the afternoon sun, they boiled upwards. In one fantastic photo I took, glorious beams of light streamed through a budding thunderhead just beyond a nearby rise. Further down the mountain, cotton candy clouds drifted lazily at or below eye level. They were far above a deep moraine valley that eventually disappeared into a bluish mist. Ice-cold water crisp air filled my lungs, and the sheer joy of being alive, right here, right now, was more intoxicating than anything I'd ever experienced. "It's great to be alive!" I yelled, my voice echoing across the valley.

From the Keyhole

Cumulus Clouds Just Over the Hill

Four hours later, I was back in the car. That night, Cindy and I celebrated by barbecuing steaks, washed down by bourbon and coke, beside a beautiful mountain stream. It was a special moment because

I had achieved a dream of 30 years and Cindy was with me to enjoy the moment. Perhaps there was still hope for us.

The flight home gave me time to reflect on the importance of holding onto a dream and doing whatever it takes to see it through. Although it had taken three years of planning and trying, I had finally stripped away the truth that our perceived limitations are nothing but lies from an insecure ego that wants us to think it is in charge. Little did I realize how strongly these revelations were soon to be tested.

Chapter 9
The Dark Night of the Soul

The Longs Peak adventures broke the lethargy I had been slipping into and opened my eyes to what could be accomplished. It also slaked my thirst for new challenges. Over the next 16 months, I began meditating daily, attending classes and reading books regarding metaphysics whenever and wherever I could.

However, the millennium ended with a thud as my plans for Cindy and I to celebrate the New Year by taking a ride in a hot air balloon devolved into an argument, the cause of which I no longer recall. Our rediscovery of one another in the Rocky Mountains the year before had been replaced, once again, by separateness. New Year's Eve, 1999, found me in bed and asleep long before the new century arrived.

The following year, I kept a 20-year vow when a distant cousin and I erected a marker for my third great-grandmother, whose forgotten grave I had discovered in an ancient cemetery in Indiana where my ancestors settled 170 years earlier. Also that summer, a spiritual teacher named Jane Hart moved to Kansas City and began offering classes on exciting topics I immensely enjoyed. Her classes were positive and personally empowering. In conjunction with the lessons I'd learned on Longs Peak, her teachings had opened my eyes to a new way of viewing the world and myself. "Belief in the possible" was taking shape.

The Christmas of 2000 was one of the best we'd ever had. Sean was a student at the University of Kansas, while Ryan was a senior in high school with plans to attend Kansas State University in the fall. My sons were turning into men before my eyes. Though it was sad to be losing my little boys, I knew the time was fast approaching to "let go" and let my sons find their ways in life.

Cindy and I didn't argue much anymore, but outside of a common devotion to our sons, we'd pretty much gone our own way. She was happy with her job working for a local psychiatrist while running her side business selling Fabergé eggs. I enjoyed being a mentor for troubled youth, working on houses for Habitat for Humanity, volunteering for a congressional candidate, and organizing an environmental committee of bank employees throughout the city. But most importantly, in the past few years I had become more tolerant as a husband and father. After years of trying to climb the corporate ladder, I'd finally come to realize that family is more important than a fancy job title or top salary. I regretted not having seen this "truth" years earlier.

As we came together for our traditional Christmas dinner, I gave thanks for all the blessings that had been bestowed on my family. Ours had been an up-and-down winding road, but things were looking better and more secure than they had been in a long time. As I gazed through the amber hue of my wine glass, I pondered my next adventure. Should I run a marathon or climb Mt. Elbert, Colorado's highest peak? Running a marathon presents a formidable challenge, but the thrill of conquering a mountain with Sean, Ryan, and Cindy offers a unique excitement. With them, anything seems possible.

The year 2001 began cold and dry. While work was busy, as always, I tried not to think about the ominous rumblings of possible job layoffs as a result of a recent merger everyone had been hearing about. One week into the new year, just before the start of the spring semester, Sean shocked everyone in the family to the core by announcing he was quitting college. The news rocked our world! He had given into the temptations of the college party scene to the extent that there wasn't enough time to fit schoolwork into his busy social schedule. Soon after leaving college, he found an apartment and got a job waiting tables at a local upscale restaurant. Sean loved the lifestyle of a handsome bachelor surrounded by pretty girls and a day's wages burning a hole in his pocket. But it was time to stand back and let him follow his chosen path in life—and the lessons it would surely bring.

In late January, I began attending another mind-expanding class by Jane Hart at Unity Church of Overland Park. Around the same time, a series of strange events started happening in the house, including knocking, bumps and noises, disappearing objects, water faucets turning on and off, and occasionally even the sound of voices. The weird events became a common joke, and whenever anything slightly out of the ordinary happened, we'd jokingly blame it on "the poltergeist."

Thursday, February 7, 2001, dawned clear and chilly. No snow was on the ground, but spring was still far away. I had a busy day ahead at work but was looking forward to the evening. Sean was coming over for a home-cooked Cajun dinner, and I eagerly anticipated the opportunity for the four of us to be together again. That morning, I inspected an apartment project in Liberty, Missouri, and on the way back to the office, stopped to buy some wine for dinner, including a bottle of Missouri apple wine that would go well with blackened redfish, red beans and rice, and gumbo.

I was head chef that evening, with Sean's help. Meanwhile, the cool sounds of a Bob Marley CD filled the house. Dinner was everything I'd hoped it would be: the food was delicious, the wine excellent. After dinner, we sat around the kitchen drinking wine, discussing the past, present, and future.

"What are your goals in life?" I asked Sean.

"I'm happy with the way things are right now," he said, "but someday, I want to either own a restaurant or be a wine representative for a large company. But for now, I love the freedom of being able to do my own thing."

"How about you, Ryan? Graduation is just a few months away, you know?"

"I'm not sure what to major in, but I definitely want to go to college, no matter what," he said.

Cindy and I smiled at one another. We were excited and proud that Ryan was going to college because he had worked really hard the past four years and made steady academic progress since junior high school.

When it came time to bring the evening to a close, I gave Sean a big hug as he put on his coat to go. After he left, Cindy went to bed, and Ryan went to his room to watch TV. I got comfy in my favorite easy chair in the upstairs living room and played more music. After a while, I dozed off, content with the world.

Around 3:30 in the morning, I woke up feeling dizzy. Rousing myself from the comfort of the chair, I went outside and sat on the front porch. The crisp, icy air felt good going into my lungs as I surveyed the deathly still nighttime scene. After a while, the chill began seeping into me, and I shuddered. With my head cleared but still dizzy, I got up and went back into the house, locking the door behind me. Slowly, I began walking up the short six stairs to our bedroom level.

The next thing I knew, I was lying at the bottom of the stairs on my stomach, sprawled across the threshold between the kitchen and the living room. For a few moments, I lay stunned. Finally, the threads of the carpet came into focus just inches from my eyes, taking on the appearance of a tiny forest world. I didn't realize then that I'd fallen backward, head over heels, down the stairs.

Cindy came rushing to my side. "What happened?" she shrieked.

Slowly, and not knowing why, I said, "The poltergeist pushed me." Staring down at me strangely in silence for a few moments, she finally said, "Well, I'm calling 911!"

"No! Just let me lie here a while. I'll be OK in a few minutes." She left the room and I tried to lift my head. It wouldn't move. Not to worry, I thought, this is much like when I had a back spasm while living in Chicago and couldn't get up from the floor for an entire night. I waited a bit, then tried to move again. Nothing. With increasing panic, I ordered my muscles to respond. They refused. Minute after minute ticked by until it became obvious that something very serious had happened to me. After mustering enough strength, I feebly called out for Cindy to call for help.

The wail of sirens filled the room, and the lights of an ambulance and fire truck reflected off the walls. Seconds later, legs were all around me. Alarmed and excited voices came from somewhere above me as paramedics discussed how best to move me. Finally, six pairs of hands slid underneath me.

Gently, these strangers lifted me above the carpet as the tiny carpet forest world disappeared, only to be replaced by a moonscape of geometric shapes created by the woven fabric covering their stretcher. Moments later, the lighted room was replaced by utter blackness and cold air as the wheels of my stretcher bumped and rumbled against the metal floor of the ambulance. Doors slammed, and away we screamed into the night.

The following hours were a blur. Strange lights, sounds, and voices were everywhere and nowhere. At the emergency ward of the hospital, my stretcher was placed on a cart and wheeled rapidly down a long corridor as I drifted in and out of consciousness. At some point, I was put into a hospital bed and a stiff brace placed around my neck. But only briefly. Soon I was zoomed away as more corridors flew by, leading to cool rooms filled with giant machines where mysterious tests were performed.

Time blurred. Finally, I was put in a room and fell asleep. The following morning Cindy came in and two serious-looking doctors wearing white coats walked into my room in the intensive care unit. Both were neurosurgeons, one much older than the other. "Mr. McCord, I'm afraid you've broken your neck between the fifth and sixth cervical, and your spinal cord has been bruised. It's called Brown-Séquard Syndrome.[1] Both of us concur that the risk of surgery is too high and it's best to let the broken bone in your neck heal in place."

Weakly, I asked, "What does this mean?"

"We're not sure yet, but it's very serious. We'll know more once the swelling has gone down. For now, try to get some rest." Everyone left the room except Cindy. Not understanding the import of what we'd just been told, we stared silently at one another. Finding nothing to say, she also left.

What a fix; only slight skin sensations and nearly completely paralyzed. A thousand questions and possible implications popped into my head: Is this the way I'll be for the rest of my life? Will I ever be able to work again? If I can't work, how will the family survive financially? Who will look after me? Cindy? Or will I be put in a nursing home?

In spite of my situation, I wasn't angry at God, myself, or anyone else. In fact, I didn't think or feel much of anything at all. Perhaps I was still in shock, or maybe it was just a continuation of how I'd always responded to a crisis—put all emotions in check. This time, however, my resolve was about to be tested as never before.

I had always been a modest person who prided himself on not having to depend upon others for much of anything. What a wake-up call! Later in the day, Cindy came with Sean and Ryan, and they sat with me for a while. Toward evening, our family physician stopped by and offered a few words of encouragement. Although he was no expert in spinal injuries, his optimism lifted my spirits. Quickly kissing me goodbye on the forehead, Cindy and the boys went home.

Alone, I stared at the back of the closed door. All was quiet except for the steady sigh of my new friend, an air respirator. Occasionally, a nurse or aide called to check on me or give me medication. Fortunately, there was cable TV to watch, and I had just enough strength in my hand to squeeze the remote control to change the channel. While watching some of my favorite shows was comforting, certain sights and sounds impacted me from that night forward. Forever after, the theme song to the show "Modern Marvels" caused me to shudder.

Staring through the glass wall of my room out onto the main ward, I sighed. What a great way to spend a Saturday night. Finally, with some time to think, the events of the past 12 hours began to surface in my mind. How could I have fallen backward down some stairs? Such a thing had never even come close to happening in my entire life! And why did I say a poltergeist had pushed me? Strange events had been occurring in the house, but what an odd statement. I resolved to have myself hypnotized someday to discover exactly what happened. The perplexing litany of questions was broken when Cindy appeared around 4 p.m. However, she had things to do and only stayed an hour or so. Around 5 p.m., a nurse's aide entered the room, set a dinner tray on a movable table, and pushed it in front of me. Shoving a fork into a fat rubber tube so I could grasp it, she handed me the weapon. Thank God my right arm works, I said to myself. The food looked and tasted equally bland. After picking at it unenthusiastically for a few minutes, I asked her to take it away. The aide left with the tray in hand, shutting the door behind her.

With nothing but a long, lonely evening to look forward to, my eyes slowly circumnavigated the room from the bag of clear IV fluid on a pole next to the bed to the long plastic tube, from the bag into my hand to the air compressor faithfully sighing away in the corner. Beyond the window wall of my room, the Intensive Care Unit was dimly lit. All of a sudden, my nose began dripping. Annoyed that there was nothing resembling a hankie nearby, I "snuffed" my nose. Big mistake! Streaks of white lightning shot throughout my brain and across my field of vision, followed by searing, blinding pain. It felt as though someone had plunged a dagger to its hilt into the right side of my neck while simultaneously putting a knife in my hand and sticking it into a 220-volt outlet. I had no idea the human body was capable of such pain.

Mindlessly, I groped for the emergency call device with my good hand. Where is it? Finally, vaguely feeling a cord, I latched onto it, causing the control box to swing wildly back and forth through empty air. A yank sent it flying up and across the bed. Inch by inch, I reeled the cord toward me. Finally, my hand collided with a solid object. I'd found it! Now, where was the call button? Desperately, I groped until I found a button, then ordered my useless fingers to push it. After missing several times, I finally succeeded. After what seemed an eternity, a male nurse came into the room. "What's the matter?" the nurse asked casually. Through gritted teeth, I tried to tell him what had happened. "I'll be back in a minute," he said expressionlessly and left.

In the silence that followed, minutes were like hours as waves of pain shot back and forth throughout my body like heat lightning across a sultry summer night sky. Finally, the aide returned. "The doctor who's on-call for the evening doesn't think your pain is related to your broken neck," he said. "We're going to give you some morphine." I stared at him in incredulous silence. Not related to the injury? Are you crazy? But the anger was confined to my mind. The only words that weakly came out of my mouth were, "This has to be related to my injury! What else could it be?" "I'm only following the doctor's orders," he shrugged, then left again. Soon, the nurse returned, holding a small bottle and a large syringe. Dully, I watched the long needle disappear into my arm, feeling nothing. "I can't believe…" I started to say, but the sentence was never finished.

Slowly, my eyes opened to a shadowy world of mysterious shapes grinning gleefully at me. From somewhere, a small light weakly illuminated a small portion of the room. Who am I? What am I? What planet is this? Bizarre shapes and colors appeared from a nightmare world in my mind's eye before disappearing, only to be replaced by new horrors. Mercifully, the netherworld spell was finally broken by a raging thirst. Seeing a cup on a nightstand near the bed, I attempted to reach for it. My right arm didn't move. Again, I commanded my arm to move. Nothing. The realization jarred me fully back to reality. Oh my God, now my right arm is paralyzed, too! Thunderstruck with fear, I remembered the call button was still in my left hand. After pressing the button as hard as I could, from far down the hall, the faint sound of an alarm from the night nurse duty station could be heard. Within seconds, a male nurse came into the room.

"Now I can't move anything!" I bewailed. He left quickly but returned before long, accompanied by another man and a portable X-ray machine. After setting it up and aiming the nozzle at my neck, the machine hummed briefly and was whisked away. Anxiously, I awaited the results.

Thirty minutes later, at 4:00 a.m., the night doctor and radiologist returned. "The broken bone in your neck has moved and pierced your spinal cord," the doctor said matter-of-factly. For several moments, I stared at him in silence. Finally, looking him in the eye, I asked softly, "Why wouldn't you believe me when I told you that nine hours ago?" The doctor's eyes briefly met mine and then dropped. "We're scheduling you for neck surgery at 11:30 tomorrow morning," he said. After they left the room, my brave front crumbled, not into fear but anger. How could the neurosurgeon on call not have realized the cause of my pain? Why didn't the duty nurse question him more or ask for a second opinion? Whatever the reason, the bone had been lodged in my spine for nine hours, much longer than if I'd been operated on that evening. How much additional damage had resulted? Fearful thoughts filled my mind: What if the surgeon makes a mistake during this delicate operation? One tiny slip, and I'll be completely paralyzed for the rest of my life. I may be anyway. How will I be able to do things with Sean and Ryan? What will happen between Cindy and me? Life as I know it will be gone forever.

One by one, the intervening hours crawled by. At 11 a.m. sharp, a team of men and women dressed in colorful scrubs and squeaky shoes entered my room, moved me onto a stretcher cart, and wheeled me down a long hallway. Once again, the ceiling world whizzed by as I closed my eyes and tried to go to a special, quiet place in my mind I had discovered during meditation.

Suddenly, I wasn't in Overland Park Regional Hospital. I was in another time and place. I soared gracefully as an eagle above a bucolic hilly forest scene. I was above a secluded area in the Lake of the Ozarks where I had hiked in happier times. I was surrounded by an iridescent glow of unseen white and gold beings flying alongside me, emanating feelings of love and protection. The feeling was familiar. Then it came back to me. This was the same feeling I'd had that night in the car in the Rockies so long ago after being let go from a job. As before, a sense of calmness came over me. Facing the most critical and dangerous moment of my life, I felt anxiety but no fear. I was comforted from a place far away yet oh-so-near. I knew the place well but couldn't quite recall the details.

The surgery room was cold. People bustled about making final preparations for the operation. A feeling of warmth followed a vague prickly sensation in my arm as the anesthesia coursed through my veins. Past, present, and future blended together, and from somewhere, the following words from an old song came to my mind: Whatever will be will be. The future's not ours to see. What will be, will be.[2]

A muffled voice broke the silence. In matter-of-fact tones, the sound of a male voice resonated with the quiet confidence of someone who knew what he was doing. It was the neurosurgeon giving post-operative instructions to his assistants. The operation was over. As the steady voice became more distinct, my eyes slowly opened to see smiling eyes behind a surgical mask. The voice behind the eyes said, "Everything went well."

Soon, ceilings flew by once again, followed by the sense of silhouetted figures bustling about. My body slid onto a different surface. Glancing sideways, I recognized my bed and room in the ICU. After a while, the bustling ceased and the room became dark. With no discernible body, I was a formless blob floating in a vast sea of energy where space, time, reality, and imagination merged into one.

Eventually, the twilight realm between worlds faded. Shadows seeped in, along with deep sighs and clicks. I resisted leaving the idyllic world where there was no pain or broken bodies. But I had no choice. Even from my floating state, I knew there were lessons to be learned and things to be accomplished in this reality. Slowly, I became aware of a denser form of energy—my physical body. Glancing about, I noticed silhouetted shapes that filled the room as an opaque shaft of light crept up a far wall. Gathering my thoughts into some semblance of order, I tried to reach for a cup of water on the nightstand with my right arm. It didn't move. What remained of the beautiful realm shattered like a porcelain vase hitting the floor as the realization of near-total paralysis stunned me.

For a long while, I lay in silent fear. Finally, the door opened and Cindy entered, followed by a nurse's aide carrying a food tray. The aide placed a bib under my chin and tried to get me to taste some cereal on a spoon. But the thought of eating was abhorrent.

"NO! Don't you understand?" I screamed. "I can't move anything. I'm ruined!" Without a response, the nurse patiently tried to get me to eat. Eventually, I took a bite of the horrid paste and then asked her to take it away. Once she was gone, I broke into a flood of curses at the doctor who had misdiagnosed what happened the night before and the 12-hour surgery that resulted. My rant finally subsided. Cindy said nothing. Suddenly, a doctor entering the room came into my field of vision.

"Am I going to be OK?" I whispered, afraid but desperate to hear his answer.

"It's still too early to know, Mr. McCord. The body's ability to recover from spinal injuries as serious as yours, with damage on two sides of the column, is very uncertain."

Cindy sat staring at nothing in particular. I wondered what she was thinking. I'm sure she wondered how she was going to manage an invalid husband who couldn't work. Perhaps she regretted our time together and how it led to this. She had undoubtedly been unhappy for years and maybe her life seemed hopeless. I wouldn't have blamed her if these were her thoughts.

From seemingly out of nowhere, a man walked into the room. It was Reverend Greg Barrette, the senior minister at Unity Church of Overland Park that I had attended since returning from Chicago. I was shocked that Greg knew, much less cared, that I was in the hospital. I was a little fish in a big pond and definitely not a large financial contributor.

"How are you, Mike? We were on our way out of town on vacation and just passing the hospital when I heard you were in the hospital. So I decided to stop by." I think both of us were amazed at the synchronicity. We talked for a while, and his words of encouragement were uplifting. Then we prayed together.

Too soon, Greg was gone. It's funny, but I don't remember much of what he said. It doesn't matter. More important was that he cared enough to stop and see me at that moment when I most needed hope. His gesture affected me more deeply than any spoken word directed to me. But beyond that, his visit caused me to rethink the way I'd viewed people for much of my life. Could it be that not everyone only looks out for themselves as I'd always thought? While I reveled in the afterglow of Greg's visit, Cindy had little to say. With no talk about the possible ramifications my paralysis could have upon our future, she patted my hand and whispered goodbye.

Alone, I tried to make some sense of all that had happened in the past 72 hours. The simple reality was that, suddenly, I was quadriplegic with a very small chance of recovery. Slowly, I mulled the word over in my mind. What exactly does it mean to be a quadriplegia? According to the dictionary, paralysis results in the partial or total loss of use of all limbs and torso. The loss is usually sensory and motor, meaning sensation and control are lost.[3]

The definition is apt to describe my condition. I couldn't move my right arm and left leg. While I could move my left arm and right leg, neither the hand nor foot responded to my mental commands. I couldn't sit up. I couldn't urinate. In short, I was a helpless invalid. What am I going to do? What will become of me? Dark visions crossed my mind. My only solace was to escape into the pleasant revelations Greg's visit brought me.

The following days brought many people into my hospital room, and a routine of sorts developed. Each morning, two young physical therapists gave me simple exercises to do. After my pathetic attempts at trying to do something, they would smile and say something cheery such as "You're doing much better today!" I knew they were lying. Stop patronizing me, I screamed inside.

Then, and for many months afterward, I was plagued with demonic questions. How could such a stupid thing happen? I could better accept being injured if it had happened while I was leading troops into battle, falling off a mountain ledge, rescuing someone from a disaster, or doing something of redeeming value, but falling down some stupid stairs in the middle of the night? Come on! If not so serious, the injury would be laughable. Regardless, what an inconceivably stupid, worthless idiot I was! Then, my anger turned toward others.

Why had the doctors not gotten me into surgery sooner? My surgery had been unnecessarily delayed at least twelve hours, and who knows how much additional damage resulted? Finally, there were deeper questions for which there were no easy answers: What did I do to deserve this fate? Was it karmic retribution for an injustice I'd committed in a former lifetime? What actually caused the fall? Was it because I had drunk wine earlier in the evening?

Was it a reaction to my blood pressure medicine? I had, after all, been having dizzy spells for several months. Or was there something else? People collapse when they pass out rather than propelling backward, right? And why had I made the strange statement right after the accident that a poltergeist had pushed me? Someday, I vowed, I will have myself hypnotized to learn the answer to these and other questions.

Each day, Cindy came to see me for an hour or so. Otherwise, except for the hospital staff, I was alone. Perplexed and hurt by Cindy's brief visits, I wondered how things had come to this between us. I knew she had never gotten over her resentment for our leaving Nebraska.

I used the time to try to rationalize my situation. While knowing little about spinal injuries, if the spinal cord was bruised, I reasoned, surely this is like any other bruise and will heal itself, won't it? And while a broken neck isn't something I would recommend for entertainment, bones heal, too. What's the big deal? I'll be fine, I tried to reassure myself. Months later, my neurosurgeon told me that only about 10 percent of people with my type of injury ever walk again.

During my seven days in the ICU, many life-and-death situations took place. One day, I heard the sound of crying. An older woman passed my door toward the elevator with the assistance of an aide. Her husband had just passed away. Another person was brought in critically injured from an auto accident. In silent witness, I watched these human dramas unfold around me. Such experiences gave me a deeper insight into the inevitability of death and the preciousness of life, something I'd ignored or taken for granted all my life. Likewise, the longer I was there, the more I understood that the nurses, nurse's aides, and hospital employees were all experiencing their own stories of fear or hope.

One day, an X-ray technician told me through shining eyes of the adventures he'd had with his sons hiking to deep blue lakes high in the South American Andes. Hanging onto his every word, I envisioned crystal clear mountain lakes surrounded by jagged snowy peaks that reached to the sky. How lucky he was to be able to fully experience every second of the limited time on earth that each of us is granted. Would I ever again experience first-hand the richness and beauty of life? Were the words correct, "What will be will be?" Do I even have a say in the matter?

Pondering these questions, I again reflected upon the topic of religion. As a small child, I thought of God as an elderly white man with a long white beard dressed in flowing white robes. I believed he was "somewhere out there" in the clouds, sitting on a throne, holding his staff, Jesus at his side. Together, they kept a running tab of your actions, particularly "sins," as the Bible defines. God was there to help you if you went to church regularly and obeyed His commandments. However, if you messed up in any way, it was dicey whether He would intervene. In my ignorance, I figured I was probably one of those sinners who hadn't made the cut and was all alone.

As a teenager, long conversations with my mother had changed my view of God and the meaning of the universe, as discussed earlier. "How," she asked, "could a God of love create such a horrible world in which everything has to eat everything else to survive? If that's what God is, I don't want any part of him." Finally, her openness to Christian Science's belief that we have the power to heal ourselves has long intrigued me. As an adult, I revolted against what I perceived as judgmental views by some religious denominations toward people who don't share their beliefs. I was also convinced that many were more concerned with maintaining the church's power and control over people than serving their well-being. In 1991, I finally began attending a Unitarian Church primarily to expose Sean and Ryan to a non-dogmatic religion.

In spite of my spiritual awakening, I still assumed that, for the most part, I was on my own in this world. But did I have the power to do it all by myself? If ever there was a time to ask for God's help, I thought now might be a pretty good time. So alone in my room one afternoon, I said aloud, God, what am I going to do to get out of this? Instantaneously, a voice came back as clear as any audible sound I'd ever heard. The answer was short and direct:

- **DO WHAT'S DOABLE WHENEVER YOU CAN**

- **WORK ON YOUR AREAS OF STRENGTH FIRST.**
- **DON'T GIVE UP (believe).**

Shocked, I whispered: Where did that come from? The message was simply and clearly well stated and there was a certainty to it that I knew represented Truth. As I slowly mulled the words over and over in my mind, I felt strangely comforted, just as I did in Colorado so many years before. But never had I been given such an immediate, direct, and powerful message. This had to be the Word of God—a roadmap to ultimate recovery. But did I have the courage to follow it?

The next time Cindy came to visit, I asked her to write the message on a piece of paper. She seemed surprised but did so as I slowly repeated the divine message to her, word for word. Afterward, I asked her to tape it on the wall beside my bed. When I left the hospital, I took the piece of paper with me, and the message became my mantra of hope. Whenever I felt discouraged or tempted to give up, I would read the words out loud. Over and over, I pondered the meaning of each word:

Do what's doable whenever you can. (But how will I know what's

doable?)

Only we can be the judge of this. One of our greatest strengths is realizing our capability and accepting it, however large or small, without reservation or judgment. Don't ask too much of yourself. Just be the best you can be.

Work on your areas of strength first. Wouldn't it be better to work on your weakest areas first? Realize your strength, whether mental, physical, or spiritual, for it's the foundation upon which your temple of desires is built. The more you concentrate on your strength, the more it will grow. As you become stronger, each task will become easier, and your confidence will soar. There are no limits to what can be accomplished, only plateaus. You must keep reaching higher. Success begets success.

Never give up. (Believe!). It is easy enough to understand but much more challenging to put into practice. Believing in accomplishing a goal and being determined to work toward it, regardless of obstacles persistently, are essential for success.

Dale Carnegie said, "If you pursue a dream long enough, pretty soon, the dream will start pursuing you."

While the answers resonated with truth, I sighed. What a long, hard road. Do I have the willpower and perseverance to do these things? Then it came to me. I had been here before. Not in bed unable to move, but here all the same. The image of a little blue train came into my mind: a little train pulling a heavy load up a mountain. The little train that nobody believed could succeed except her. The little train that wouldn't quit and kept telling herself, over and over again against all odds, "I think I can" – "The Little Engine that Could,"[5] the record that I'd listened to as a small child until I finally wore the record out. *She did it, but can I?*

Chapter 10
A New Reality

Shortly after breakfast, a doctor and nurse entered my room and broke the quiet, cave-like spell it had come to be.

"Mr. McCord, you need to decide where you want to go to continue your physical rehabilitation. There are two places in Kansas City. Both are good, but one is known for making its patients work harder than the other. Which one do you want to go to?"

The decision was easy. I wanted to be challenged in every way possible, and that's what they did at the Rehabilitation Institute. So the Rehabilitation Institute it was.

Shortly after lunch the following chilly and cloudy Friday, more kind strangers lifted me from my bed and placed me on a flat cart. Out the door and down the hall, we went to a waiting ambulance. The hospital ceilings whirled by for one last time, only to be replaced by an ambulance ceiling. I was becoming quite a connoisseur of the finer points of ceilings.

After a 20-minute bumpy ride, the ambulance came to a stop. The back doors opened, letting in a whoosh of cold air as harsh daylight blinded my eyes. The wheels of a stretcher rumbled below me, sending vibrations that were sensed but not felt as it was pulled out of the ambulance and placed onto the ground. There was more rumbling as we went through sliding doors and, a few feet later, into an elevator. Such was the introduction to my new home, the Rehabilitation Institute of Kansas City, Missouri, shortly after 1 p.m. on a gloomy Friday, February 16, 2001.

My room was on the second floor near the nurse's station. It was starkly furnished with no wall art or even cheerily painted walls. There were two empty beds so naturally I chose the one closest to the only window in the room. "At least I can look at the sky," I thought. How wonderful it would be to see the sky again. It's funny how we take little things such as the sky for granted. But once gone they're suddenly not so "little."

Three aides hoisted me into the bed where I was to spend much of my time for the next seven weeks. Following a lot of bustling, Cindy and everyone else left and I was alone. The deafening silence was filled only by the sound of blood rushing in my ears. The place had an utterly depressing and institutional feel, made even more so by a large school clock hanging in the middle of a ten-foot wall directly in front of me. As I watched, the second hand crept almost imperceptibly around the dial. It was 1:33 p.m. I looked away and tried to think of other things: "What drab colors. Maybe some new curtains might help. I wonder whether it will snow tonight? Finally, I had to look—1:34. Arrgh!" Now transfixed by the electrical beast, the second hand grew gargantuan. One second passed. Then another, then another. I had to think of something else before this clock from hell, which by now was openly mocking me, drove me from an "institute" to an "asylum"!

To escape, my mind wandered back to that lazy fall afternoon in my bedroom so long ago when, as a boy of eight, I lay in bed watching another clock while similarly contemplating each second that passed. How ironic it is that two situations can be so similar yet different. But the truths revealed by both incidents remained: time is relative to how we perceive it. Each moment can be as fleeting or as excruciatingly long as we wish it to be. It also may be either heaven or hell, as we so choose. What's remarkable is that we have the choice. We're in control of every second of our lives. I finally had an answer to a question posed long ago in a song written by Jim Croce: you can "catch time in a bottle."

Well, I thought, if my mind is in control of time, it might as well be in charge of it. This damned clock has to go, or I'm going to be a stark-raving loony by dinnertime! When a nurse came in, I asked if she would move the clock so I wouldn't have to see it.

"No," she huffed indignantly. "Important decisions such as this must be approved by the maintenance department!"

What BS, I thought! Later in the day, a male nurse's aide came into my room. Again, I pleaded my case to move the clock.

"Sure," he said casually, removing the clock and putting it on top of a closet on the other side of the room. It was my first victory in what seemed a long time. I chuckled slyly to myself; there's more than one way to skin a cat around here. It was a lesson I didn't plan to forget.

I turned on the TV that night and got my next shock. No cable. Oh my God, anything but that! I couldn't stomach the thought of having to listen to the mindless chatter on most commercial channels. I'd been looking forward to watching programs on the few TV channels I could stand, such as History, Discovery, and the Travel Channel, as a way to escape reality for at least a while in this bleak place. How am I going to get through this? I groaned.

Ironically, being unable to watch television turned out to be one of the greatest blessings of my time at the Institute. The solitude and lack of distractions allowed me to explore deeper areas of my consciousness than ever before. In the ensuing weeks, I contemplated God, the universe, and the true meaning of life at every opportunity. My meditations became more prolonged and more profound than ever before. I traveled to beautiful, exciting places in my mind: fantasia worlds overflowing with exquisite colors. The sages were right: *what truly matters is love, living in the now, and appreciating simple blessings*. I felt most of these blessings had been taken from me "in the wink of an eye." I was only beginning to realize how fortunate I'd been to have them most of my life.

Several strange events took place during those first days in the rehab hospital. After the light had been turned out the first night when I was trying to sleep, I heard what sounded like someone getting into the other bed in the room. Noises persisted from that side of the room for about an hour. I'll never know whether a staff worker had slipped into the room to nap in the unoccupied bed or something else.

Following a bland dinner spoon-fed by a nurse's aide the next night, I stared absently out the window from my bed. The hours passed. Eventually, someone shut off the lights and closed the door to my room. In darkness and silence, I continued to stare out the window, unable to sleep. Then something remarkable happened. A flurry of tiny white objects began swirling outside the window around the pane. Snow? None had been predicted. I squinted to see the growing blizzard of activity better. Then things got even stranger. Slowly, at first, tiny objects began streaming through the window into the room itself. They increased in intensity, and before long, millions were pouring into the room in long streams of light. At times, they looked like waves, and at other times, like particles. For a long time, I tried to rationalize what I was seeing. Finally, it dawned on me. They're photons, light energy! Could such a thing be possible? At that moment, "how" didn't matter as I marveled at the incredible beauty of this strange sight. How had I missed this astonishing phenomenon all my life? Although I never again experienced this fantastic phenomenon, years later, I learned that, while rare, the human brain is capable of seeing light photons.[1] Apparently, I'd never slowed down enough to see something that was there all along.

Cindy came to visit on Sunday afternoon. As she and an aide adjusted the Venetian blinds while I watched from my wheelchair, I caught some movement out of the corner of my right eye. Turning to the right, about a foot away and head high with me, was an opaque light about the size of a basketball shimmering like a piece of cellophane in the wind. As I stared dumbfounded, the silent mass slowly began moving toward the hallway door. Eventually, it disappeared from my field of vision. I told Cindy and the aide what I'd seen, but they simply laughed and said it was my imagination. Was it a ghost, a reflection, or were they right?

The final event seems funny now but certainly wasn't so back then. Monday evening, a nurse's aide removed my neck brace in preparation for showering me. Two aides moved me from my bed into a wheelchair and then wheeled me into an open shower stall in the bathroom. While I couldn't actually feel the water, knowing what it was lifted my spirits. Afterward, it seemed different when they began putting my neck brace on. Indignantly, I asked, "Who switched my neck brace?" Not only did the color seem different, but it was uncomfortable. No matter how much they tried to convince me it was the same brace, I wouldn't believe them. It took me several days to accept that it was the same brace as before.

I learned later that people deprived of sensory stimulation sometimes suffer from illusions. So, were my experiences illusions? Obviously, the incident regarding the neck brace was a figment of my imagination, but what about the others? Were they also my imagination, or had I glimpsed another reality? I'll never know for sure, but nothing could have been more real. Perhaps if we slowed down a bit and really opened our eyes, we'd surely be amazed at the wonders that would be revealed.

Monday morning, three days after entering the world of institutionalized living, three men in white coats entered my room shortly after breakfast. They were led by Dr. Anderson, the Institute's lead physician. Dr. Anderson was in his late 30s with a kind and easy-going demeanor. He was also a Nebraskan like me, and we formed an immediate bond. Before long, the conversation turned to the state's football team, the Cornhuskers, for which every Nebraskan is a fan. After a while, I finally got the nerve to ask the question that had been constantly on my mind the past week: "What is my prognosis?" For what seemed an eternity, Dr. Anderson stood in silence. Finally, he said quietly, "Optimistic."

I sighed in relief. It didn't occur to me till later that "optimistic" could mean many things, none of which require walking. It's probably just as well. For days, I'd been telling myself I WOULD walk again, not that I wouldn't, so naturally, I positively interpreted his vague prognosis.

Still, Dr. Anderson's words meant everything to me: I better appreciated his diplomatic choice of words once I fully understood the severity of my injury. What good would it have been if he'd said something like, "You're never going to walk again," or even what he already knew: that only around ten percent of people with my type of injury ever walk again. Would I have taken an unfavorable prognosis as a challenge, making me even more determined to succeed? Or would I have sunk into despair?

As Gregg Braden wrote in "The Spontaneous Healing of Belief," the slightest hint from a physician that a treatment may not work can have devastating consequences for its success. It can be so disturbing, in fact, that it can kill. *According to Braden, word, expression, and even the body language a doctor uses when talking to a patient can be critical to a patient's recovery because his belief is that most, but not all, healing begins in the mind.*[2] *Further, doctors should never tell their patients they can't do something or that their prognosis is hopeless, he said, because medical science is only beginning to understand the incalculable importance of the patient's state of mind: attitude, faith, belief, determination, and commitment to recover.*[3]

And so it began. As soon as the doctors left the room that Monday morning, I started my first day of therapy. There were three separate sessions, each lasting about an hour, all of which were held in a large room on the first floor with the appearance and feel of a small gymnasium. That first day, an aide wheeled me to the therapy room for the only time. Taking the elevator to the first floor and down a long hallway, we entered the therapy room.

The sight amazed me. The room was filled with people of all ages, shapes, and sizes, from children to teenagers to adults to senior citizens. All had earnest looks on their faces as they struggled to do the things being asked of them by about a half dozen therapists. Some patients lay on mats, straining to lift a leg or move their toes. Others held rails or walked obstacle courses. A man was sitting on a long table, struggling to shove blocks through correctly shaped openings. I'd join the next group of patients; meanwhile, I and several other people in wheelchairs sat like autos on a factory assembly line, awaiting our turns. The efficiency of the place would have pleased Henry Ford.

Finally, the time came for my session. I was introduced to my primary physical therapist, Randy, who would work on major motor skills. My occupational therapist was Cathy, who would work on finer motor skills such as hand dexterity. Many other therapists would be assisting them. Following introductions, Randy sat me upright on a mat. I fell over like a sack of potatoes onto my side. He propped me up again—the same result. Next, I was laid on my back, placing my right arm behind my head. "Lift your arm," a therapist said. I strained and grunted with all my might, but the arm would not budge. An hour or so later, the session came to an end. Exhausted and dejected, I slowly wheeled down the long hallway to my room on the third floor. Following two more equally unproductive sessions, the day mercifully ended.

Compared to my previous life, quadriplegia was unfathomable. I couldn't sit up, dress, shave, brush my teeth, or wash. Before the injury, I'd joked with a coworker that I would never get a massage because I didn't want some guy I didn't know touching me. On the other hand, if it were a lady masseuse touching me, something sexually embarrassing might happen. In the coming weeks, my pride became a joke as every orifice, crease, crack, and cavity in my body was examined, probed, or manipulated by people I'd never seen before and probably would never see again. Talk about an ego-deflating irony! But there wasn't a choice. Truthfully, I was extremely grateful to all the selfless individuals willing to do the thankless tasks I was suddenly unable to do for myself. What wonderful angels of mercy! But was I going to have to depend upon other people to do these things for the rest of my life? No, I screamed inside: it can't be!

Regardless of my resolution, doubts about my ability to overcome the curse of quadriplegia crept into my mind as I played the day's therapy failures over and over again in my mind. After a blasé dinner that first night after therapy, it eventually came time to sleep. "Leave the window shades open," I whispered to the nurse. "I don't want to lose my only connection to the natural world." Sleep was impossible, so I stared at the stars in the night sky hour after hour. Eventually, dawn approached, and the sky began to change from black to gray to rose-colored hues as the morning sun rose. Finally, the sun peaked above the horizon, the sky turning slate green. Within minutes, a cold, pale blue deepened as the sun rose higher in the eastern sky. After a while, tiny white clouds formed here and there, and, in the far distance, tiny specs—birds—swam on an ocean current of blue.

As I gazed mesmerized through sleep-deprived eyes, suddenly, the sky and everything else in the world took on the glow of a miracle. Within seconds, things I had scarcely noticed before the injury became more exquisite than words could express. From the threads in my sheets to the stars in the night sky, all glowed with divinity. Even the sun's reflection on the sand in the bricks outside my window became the eye of God looking into mine.

That morning, I also began to "see" inside others: how lonely or afraid we are and how much we all need one another. I realized how sometimes even our smallest gestures of kindness can affect the lives of others in ways that we may never know. Overwhelmed by the beauty of this universe and these revealed Truths, tears of gratitude welled in my eyes. From this place of gratitude, I gave thanks for the things I still had—the ability of rational thought, of being able to hear and to see—because there were people only a few feet away from me who didn't have these blessings. God had opened my eyes to the miracle of His universe, and I was forever changed. **I am convinced that in that instant of time—at the exact moment when I turned away from fear and opened my heart to unconditional love—my healing began.**

While I didn't know it at the time, *A Course in Miracles* says the same thing: "A broken body shows the mind has not been healed. Who forgives (lets go of judgment and fear) is healed."[4]

I began the second day of therapy with a new vision of myself and the world around me. I awoke long before the aide arrived with my breakfast tray at 6:15. Oh, how I relished those quiet moments in the dark before an aide came, safe from the increasing activity in the hallway outside my closed door. The hospital was waking up, signaling the start of another long, pain-filled day that would challenge my resolve over and over again. I dreaded the thought of even trying to move, knowing that even the slightest twitch of a muscle would send an electrical charge of pain shooting throughout my body.

The inevitable, however, could only be delayed a short while. Before long, the door to my room would be opened gently, an aide entering with a breakfast tray on a cart. After raising my bed, the aide would place a service tray in front of me and on it my breakfast. Because I had so little control over the only hand that would move, tasks such as taking the lid off the plate, opening the plastic containing straws and utensils, and pushing the straw into a carton of juice or milk were monumental challenges. But through it, I learned the virtue of patience over frustration and anger at my clumsy, non-responsive hands and arms. I also learned to be resourceful—how to cheat to make things easier. For example, I calculated how to situate everything on the tray to economize effort. I learned that teeth are an advantageous mechanism and can be used for all kinds of things, such as opening cellophane, grasping, and holding objects steadily so I could push eating utensils into a slotted rubber pad with my weak and clumsy hands. Once inserted, I held onto the fat rubber pad and transported food from the plate to my mouth. Usually, an aide helped open the lids of milk cartons and juice containers. I gave thanks for each small favor.

Following the fifteen minutes allotted for breakfast, an even more difficult task awaited: dressing myself. Under the therapist's watchful eye, I plunged into a seemingly impossible task. Every act became a significant test of willpower to move my turgid limbs. Seemingly trivial tasks required a Herculean effort of teeth-gritting, pain-filled determination. Pulling a sock over my foot required repeated attempts as my limp fingers failed repeatedly in their task. Each step was a major challenge and each success a momentous victory. But there was no time for rest or celebration: the real work of the day was about to begin!

Two aides would hoist me from the bed to a wheelchair. I rolled myself into the elevator. Sometimes, it took several jabs to push the button hard enough to start the elevator down two floors to the main level. Then I'd wheel myself down the long hallway to the therapy room that constantly buzzed with activity.

In the days to follow, my therapists continued trying to get me to sit up and raise my right arm over my head while lying on my back on a mat. Randy repeatedly tried to help me sit up, but despite his efforts to position me well on the mat, I would immediately flop onto my side as soon as he released his hold. Discouragement doesn't do justice to how I felt. Why not put a flower in each ear and use me as a doorstop, I thought.

One day after another passed by. Then it happened. One morning I remained in a sitting position after Randy had let go of me. It was the first sign that my motor skills were starting to respond, ever so slightly, to neurological commands. It was a moment I'll never forget.

Another arduous task was trying to raise my right arm while lying on my back. As an occupational therapist watched dispassionately, I grimaced in pain with pursed lips and shut eyes trying to raise my right arm. Time after time, session after session, the arm refused to budge, leaving me writhing in pain and failure. One day, however, the arm rose slightly—the next day a little more. Still, with what felt like a 50-pound weight strapped to it, I doubted I'd ever be able to raise my arm much further.

It was during an afternoon session about a week later, as I was grunting and grimacing as usual, when the arm unexpectedly sailed over the top of my head and plopped loudly on the cot beside me. For a few seconds, the therapy room was dead silent. Then, every therapist in the room burst into cheers.

Most days between therapy sessions, I sat in my wheelchair, looking out the window of my room, my only lifeline to the outside world. One morning that first week, as I sat staring idly out the window as usual, I noticed the tops of two giant cottonwood trees far in the distance, about three-fourths of a mile away. As a kid, I'd always loved trees and planted them wherever I could. For over an hour, I admired every nuance of their majestic bare limbs, limbs that had taken years to grow into uniquely shaped contortions from the tips of their branches to the bottoms of their mighty trunks. I longed for summertime and the ability to lean against one of those gentle giants, listening to the wistful sigh of their leaves in a gentle breeze. Looking closer, I perceived two dark figures circling above the trees and landing in the topmost branches. Crows. A few minutes later, they took off and disappeared into the distance. What freedom! The freedom to soar with the wind and casually observe the world as it passed below. I lived vicariously through those wonderfully free black crows for the next six weeks.

Five hours of therapy daily left me exhausted and groaning in pain far into the night. However, there still were times when there wasn't much to do, so I asked Cindy to bring me some motivational tapes. Over and over, I listened to their messages: have faith, pray, maintain positive thoughts, visualize your dreams, affirm, never give up, and believe anything is possible through the powers of the mind. Others gave inspirational examples of people who had overcome similar obstacles. The message was becoming like a drumbeat.

There was also a lot of time to think, reflect, and ponder. I began reliving something that happened around 1996 when I first became engrossed in spirituality and quantum mechanics. One day back then, after struggling for a couple of years to make sense of everything, I had what I can only describe as an "aha" moment. The revelation hit me like a thunderbolt!

Science has discovered many things since the 1920s regarding how the universe operates at both the physical and subatomic levels, only confirming what religion has taught for eons. The difference was that each side used different words to describe the same phenomenon. I laughed, realizing that both were too stubborn to see what had been staring them in the face all along. Things I'd not understood for a lifetime suddenly became clear: the world as we know it is not real but rather an illusion shaped by our individual and collective beliefs. "Consciousness" is an integral part of the universe just as much as matter and energy. As such, each of us has unlimited power to manifest the reality we choose. Throughout history, sages have repeatedly tried to tell us this truth; however, only a few have discovered the "secret" of bringing forth this divine power that we all possess.[5,6]

Through these things, I began to see how prayer works from a scientific standpoint. Everything vibrates; if consciousness can alter these vibrations, it might change our physical bodies and the world. Could this explain the occurrence of what we term 'miracles,' including miraculous healings? This realization leads to another: all faith-based religions might hold truth. Despite their diverse teachings, faith itself could be the fundamental key.[7,8] As comedian George Carlin once said, "Hey man, it doesn't matter if you worship Wilt Chamberlain's socks. Faith is what matters!"[9]

I laughed at the irony of the revelation. For years, I'd clucked smugly at what I thought was blind, superstitious faith in God and prayer on the part of organized religions. But now I saw they'd been right all along. The joke was on me. Faith and prayer work, and through them, all things are possible, just as Jesus told us time after time. I believe there are many paths to God, and the one that works best for you is the correct path. Because of this, no one has the right to criticize another person's spiritual path.

The Rehab Institute was a vital health facility for people from the inner city. Patients came from many walks of life and were there for all kinds of reasons, including strokes, drug overdoses, automobile accidents, debilitating diseases, and victims of gun violence. Sadly, many didn't have health insurance and their only resource was charity by organizations such as the Rehab Institute and United Way. How is it possible that a country as rich and powerful as the United States does not have a universally available and affordable healthcare system? I fumed.

It was heartbreaking when some patients were forced to stop coming to therapy for making bad choices, such as coming to therapy high on drugs. Additional treatment could have had an immensely positive impact on their physical conditions and quality of life. I came to know each of these people well, and even though some had made bad choices in life, I saw the beauty they all possessed inside.

At the Institute, family therapy sessions were divided between five hours of daily physical and occupational work, interspersed several times a week with group encounters and one-on-one meetings with a psychologist to acclimate us to our new way of life.

At the end of each session, I was put back into my wheelchair and wheeled myself back to my room where I stared absently out the window at Trinity Lutheran Hospital across the street, waiting for either the next session to start or my evening meal. Often, I'd ask the aide to put a cassette into my portable tape player and then have to call to change to another. I'm sure my requests became annoying over time.

Many revelations came to me during those times. Sometimes, insights would pop into my head, and I'd wonder, where did that come from? Other times, they came from conventional sources such as "How to Know God" by Deepak Chopra. The message was simple: people perceive God in the way that best coincides with their belief and understanding. Chopra said there are seven different understandings of God which form the basis of all religions. Each is correct in its own right because God is all things to all people. The message helped me realize that God works at any level of understanding by releasing fear and replacing it with love, infinite possibilities open to us.

I also spent countless hours listening to other tapes with positive and inspirational messages, such as 4T Prosperity Prosperity[11] and Chicken Soup for the Soul.[12] Their messages were precisely what I needed to hear.

Whenever I had the opportunity, I would sit with my eyes closed, meditating or visualizing myself strong and tall and walking again while drumming a consistent message into my psyche: anything is possible if you believe and keep working toward your goal. Before beginning a visualization session, I'd choose where I was "going," shut my eyes, set the intention, and clear my mind. Before long, I was experiencing every step of the journey with a sense of freedom I'd seldom felt in "real" life. What glorious adventures! Sometimes, the sun would warm my face with the wind blowing through my hair as I traversed high alpine meadows with snow-covered peaks towering above in silent sentinel. Another favorite was strolling down a secret, sun-dappled country lane winding through a protective forest. The sun shone through leaves high in the trees above while the rich, earthy smell of moist soil mingled with the scent of apple blossoms from a nearby orchard. On other occasions, I visualized working out with weights, my arms and legs rippling with strength.

When I wasn't listening to tapes or doing a visualization meditation, I'd put in additional "soul work time" in the form of "regular" meditations, during which I tried to empty my mind of all thoughts. As I sank into oblivion, a deep sense of calm and well-being descended over me. During these times, various scenes or insights popped into my mind, from answers to mundane day-to-day issues to significant revelations about life and the world around me. My reflections continued into the night as I stared into the blackness of space.

But things weren't always so serene or beautiful. One night, I suffered a brain seizure. Shortly after dinner, as I was resting in my bed, the world suddenly began to spin and I was overcome with nausea. Within seconds, I started losing consciousness, but just as the world began to fade, I found the monitor pad and pressed the emergency call button. A nurse rushed into the room, then a second. Physically, they forced me backward against my will while pushing my head lower to prevent me from swallowing my tongue. Eventually, the roller coaster experience began to subside. I learned later that a sudden constriction of a vein in my neck caused the seizure. Although it never happened again, it was a wake-up call to the seriousness of my condition. Years later, I learned I had suffered a minor stroke.

Two weeks after entering the Rehab Institute, Cindy brought Sean and Ryan to visit. It was wonderful to see them again. Both were doing well, Sean in his job as a waiter and Ryan in his last year of high school. I learned that Ryan had recently met a girl named Angela whom he liked a lot and was seeing regularly. I also learned that Sean had broken up with his long-time girlfriend, Stacy.

Before long, I began receiving cards, letters, and flowers, some from people I barely knew. As with Gregg Barrette's unexpected visit to the hospital, I was shocked at the outpouring of support. I simply couldn't understand why anyone would bother sending anything to me. Although I was a hard nut to crack, people were showing me by their actions that my thinking about them for oh-so-long had been wrong.

Around this time, I began noticing an odd electric sensation. It started at the base of my feet and then quickly shot upward throughout my body. I didn't understand what was happening, but somehow, I knew it was something important. Much later, I learned that Jane Hart, my spiritual mentor, had been leading healing meditations directed toward me during her classes at Unity during these same hours. I'm convinced those electric sensations were healing energy from them and others. It's since been scientifically proven that distant healing works.[13,14,15,16]

As I sat in my room in my wheelchair shortly after lunch one day during my second week at the Rehab Institute, the telephone rang. I leaned over to reach the phone a few feet away and even further to pick up the receiver. Finally, grasping the receiver, I said hello to a high executive with my employer calling from Charlotte, North Carolina. What an honor! We had a nice chat for a few minutes when suddenly the phone slipped out of my hand and fell to the floor. What an embarrassment!

Desperately, I reached for the cord, clenching my teeth around it, with the idea of pulling it two inches at a time, tucking the excess under my chin, and then pulling again until I could grab it with my hand. Excellent idea, but while reaching for the phone, I went over the side of the wheelchair and dangled precariously without enough strength to straighten myself. All I could see was the floor and part of one wheel of the chair. As I hung suspended in space, I could faintly hear the executive's voice chatting away merrily to no one on the phone. After struggling for at least a minute, I somehow managed to get the phone to my ear and tried to pick up on the conversation. But even after retrieving the phone, I continued hanging over the edge of the wheelchair, which was close to toppling over, sending me flopping on the floor. Throughout the rest of our conversation, I did my best to maintain a normal sound in my voice. Mercifully, the call finally came to an end. I have no idea what we talked about, but I bet she wondered why there were such long pauses on the other end of the line.

One night a new phenomenon manifested itself, but sensory deprivation wasn't even a possibility this time. As I lay fitfully in the darkened room trying to soothe my aching right arm, "something" entered the room. Invisible to the naked eye, it sat quietly on the left side of my bed near my head. I couldn't tell if the presence was male or female, but whatever it was, it knew me as well as I knew myself. Somehow, I knew we'd known each other for eons. A deep sense of love emanated from this Holy being that only wanted the very best for me. I had this experience at other significant moments in my life and had come to think of it as my best friend. Whatever one chooses to call it: God, Jesus, Holy Spirit, Allah, or guardian angel, its love and strength helped me immeasurably during those dark days. Although I no longer sense my ethereal companion's loving presence as profoundly as I did back then, I know it is still with me.

Although Cindy didn't come daily, we usually talked on the phone. I told her about each and every experience that took place. While never poo-pooing the more extraordinary things that were going on, she never fully embraced them. However, she was a great comfort to my parents in Nebraska by keeping them informed of my progress.

Several times a night, I was awakened by a team of night-duty nurses who changed my catheter bag and "turned" me, as I was susceptible to body sores. I can still hear their soft words: "One, two, three, turn; one, two, three, turn," followed by the perception of my body changing position.

Late one evening, well past midnight, unable to sleep as usual, I struck up a conversation with Sarah, a nurse on the graveyard shift, after she'd finished her chores. While I couldn't see her face, her silhouette was profiled against the light from the hallway behind her, a sight I'll never forget. The rest of the hospital was deadly quiet at this late hour as I listened in rapt attention to an amazing story. In 1979, her nephew, whose last name was Vandana, had just graduated from high school. He was in a terrible car accident and left completely paralyzed. His spinal cord had been crushed; the doctors told him there was no chance he'd ever walk again. He had played high school football and had led an active life.

Devastated by the event, young Mr. Vandana was admitted to the same Rehabilitation Institute in Kansas City, where he remained for nearly a year. The staff urged him not to waste his time trying to walk again but rather to concentrate on practical matters such as learning how to dress, feed himself, and do household chores. He refused to listen; he was determined to walk again no matter what anybody else said. Every day for months, he worked to the point of exhaustion, oftentimes staying in the therapy gym long after everyone else had gone home for the day. One day, to everyone's surprise, his legs moved a little bit. Encouraged, Vandana continued to work harder, and slowly, very slowly, his mobility began to return. Time wore on, and he could support himself with crutches when he was dismissed a year later. The young man walked upright out the door of the hospital to the utter amazement of the medical staff. But this form of walking wasn't good enough, and Vandana continued to work just as hard once he got home.

More time passed. Eventually, it became easier for him to walk. One day, to the amazement of his family, he threw away one of the crutches. A few months later, he tossed aside the other one. His ability to walk left everyone associated with the case flabbergasted. Mr. Vandana had far exceeded what any of the so-called experts thought possible. However, just walking again wasn't good enough for him. He had always dreamt of being an Air Force fighter pilot regardless of the physical rigors required to be admitted as a candidate. On and on, he pushed himself to become ever stronger and more agile. Finally, the magical day came when he was accepted into the Air Force Academy at Colorado Springs, where he graduated as a pilot. Nurse Sarah told me her nephew had retired the prior year following a 25-year career flying F-16 Fighting Falcons.

As I lay listening to Sarah's story, her face silhouetted against the light from the hallway, my heart raced. What a testament to the human spirit! Was it possible that I could fully recover as well, a low-functioning Class C Quadriplegic[17] who could not even sit up initially? It was all up to me.

Chapter 11
Waters Deep, Waters Wide

Each day blended seamlessly into the next. Although the schedule varied a little daily, it always included two physical therapy sessions, two occupational therapies, and occasionally a group session. There were six hours of therapy a day, not counting the extra time I spent on my own afterward. My therapists were friendly but pretty much all business. Every day, they pushed me to try to do more. But they didn't have to push very hard. I was a willing patient and would have continued working into the night if they had let me. As it was, I would keep trying to move something—a foot, a toe, a finger, a hand—anything, during the evening hours.

The generally accepted opinion of the medical community is that most recovery from a spinal injury, if it's going to happen, will take place during the first six months following the injury. Some additional recovery will occur for another six months, but very little after that.

One afternoon, after a long day of therapy, as I was slowly wheeling myself toward the elevator to my room, I noticed a room I had never paid much attention to. It was full of computer terminals. Although tired and anxious to get back to my bed, the words I'd received in the Intensive Care Unit kept coming back to me: Do what's doable whenever you can. What's more important than doing something right now, I wondered. Go "veg out" in my room or work on my finger dexterity? Without a second thought, I turned my wheelchair to the left and wheeled into the small computer room. Shyly, I asked the woman in charge if she would set me up on a computer. She agreed.

Before long, I was staring at a monitor showing a series of typing games. All looked silly, but I finally decided on one with a picture of a frog sitting on a lily pad in the middle of a stream. The goal was to type the word that appeared at the top of the screen before the frog was swept down the river. Each time you typed the word correctly, the frog jumped to the next lily pad, letting out an anemic "ribbit." If you misspelled the word, an annoying buzzer would go off. The objective was to correctly type as many words as you could within a two-minute period. For each word spelled correctly, a point was added. For each incorrect word, a point was deducted. Hmm, this might be fun, I thought, so I jabbed at the timer button. Within seconds, it became evident that my hands were nothing more than lobster claws. Futilely, I banged on the keyboard trying to find the right key like a monkey, hoping a piece of banana might drop into my mouth if I got it right. Occasionally, I heard a weak little "ribbit" as the cartoon frog jumped to the next lily pad. Woohoo! After the game ended two minutes later, I eagerly awaited the results. After 30 seconds of anxiety, the results flashed on the screen. Six words a minute? You gotta be kidding me! Disgusted, I played the game repeatedly until my hands stopped working. But six words per minute remained my high score for the day. With a deep groan, I went back to my room vowing to do battle another day against the mocking little frog.

The next time I played the game, I typed eight words per minute. Wow, maybe I'll make it to 20 in a couple of years. But the game was a challenge and kind of fun, so each day I wheeled myself into the computer room and tried to beat the previous day's score. Usually, but not always, I showed some improvement from the day before. Unfortunately, as my test scores improved, so did my annoyance at the cyber-frog and his ribbits! Doing my best to ignore the lame little frog, by the time I was dismissed from the Rehab Institute six weeks later, I was up to 53 words per minute!

About ten days after being admitted to the Institute, I stood up beside my wheelchair during a therapy session. Everyone was astonished! Seeing other people at an equal height rather than towering above me was strange. In fact, the entire world took on a new perspective—one that I'd quickly forgotten. The following day, I took a few baby steps as Randy held tightly to a safety belt around my waist. On the third day, I toddled a little farther. However, after about ten steps or so, black spots suddenly appeared before my eyes. I broke into a cold sweat and went down in a heap onto the floor, twisting a knee and bruising a shoulder in the process. A few days later, I passed out a second time, then a third.

Quickly, I gained a notorious reputation among the therapists. No one wanted to work with me for fear I'd "go down" on their watch. Could this tendency to suddenly lose consciousness be related to why I had passed out the night I broke my neck, I wondered? I vowed to be hypnotized someday to try to find the answer.

Another task the therapists seemed to enjoy "torturing" me with was trying to pick up tiny objects, such as push pins, and put them into holes or to stack one block on top of the other. This was maddeningly tricky because of the turgidity of my hands and fingers. More than once I cheated and used my teeth when no one was looking!

In spite of such frustrations, from the earliest days in the Institute, I told pretty much anyone who would listen that someday I was going to run again and climb mountains. "And when I do," I would say, "I'm going to send you a picture." My bold proclamations were met with amused silence. Although no one ever flatly refuted my goals, they clearly didn't believe such things were possible. Perhaps Randy summed up their feelings best when he mused, "Why don't we try to get you walking first!"

Dinner was served around 5:30 each evening. Patients could choose from several entrées. The food was pretty good, but after a while it became monotonous once I realized that the menu repeated itself like clockwork every seven days.

Two or three times a week, at my insistence, an aide would shave me after the evening meal. Every person on the staff dreaded this ritual because it meant they had to remove my neck brace and were afraid I'd break like a piece of china.

Twice a week, I was placed in my wheelchair and rolled into a flowing shower stall—kind of like a car going through a car wash. I didn't mind because by now I was used to being treated like a mannequin. Besides, the water felt good!

My evening care came to an end around 8 p.m., no doubt to the relief of the overworked staff. At last, there was time to listen to a cassette tape or watch a movie Cindy had brought. Frequently, I wished she was there to watch a movie with me, but she apparently had other things to do.

Friday nights were special. That was the night Cindy brought me the fast food of my choice. Although I rarely ate fast food at home, I eagerly anticipated such delicacies as Taco Bell or Long John Silver and the change of pace they represented. Usually, Cindy would stay for about an hour or so. Twice, however, she brought two special visitors to see me: our Boston Terrier, Darby, and one of our kitties, Taka. I was as ecstatic to see them as they were to see me. When Darby saw me, he was at first delirious with happiness, kissing me violently with his wet tongue until my face was a soggy mess. But after a while, he began mixing a few light nips to my chin along with the kisses along with a slight growl to let me know he wasn't very happy about me not being home with him.

I talked on the phone several times a week with Mom and Dad in Nebraska. Hearing their voices brought a tremendous sense of comfort that helped put life back into perspective. While they couldn't come to Kansas City to see me for health reasons, knowing they were with me in spirit meant everything.

Another visitor was Joe Gardner, a distant relative. The prior year, we had driven to Indiana to erect a headstone for one of our common ancestors, fulfilling my twenty-year vow since discovering the broken and forgotten headstone of my third-great-grandmother nearly two inches underground at an ancient cemetery in Daviess County, Indiana. Doing so had bonded us with the satisfaction of knowing we had resurrected the forgotten memory of a brave pioneer woman who was crucial to our family's history. The lesson was clear: do what you desire when you have the chance because no one knows what tomorrow may bring.

Dr. John, a psychiatrist for whom Cindy worked, visited several times. We talked for hours about weighty topics such as the mind-body connection and the meaning of life. One night, I asked Dr. John what he thought about the placebo effect, something observed in medical science for many years. The placebo effect occurs when a patient's symptoms improve due to their expectation or belief in the treatment, even though the treatment has no known medical benefit. "Well," he said, "science considers the placebo effect to be a short-term response to a suggestion from an authority figure."

If this is true, I said, why have so many people been healed permanently by taking a sugar pill that they believed was real medicine? Clearly, something else was going on—wasn't there?

"Science really doesn't have an answer as to why this happens," he responded, "so they just write it off as a medical anomaly."

"Can't doctors see the obvious," I asked. "The answer is as plain as the noses on their faces. The mind is the mechanism that heals the body, and healing is triggered by the power of belief."

"I don't know," Dr. John shrugged.

Later, I asked myself again why a placebo works for some people but not others. And why do some people recover from terminally diagnosed illnesses when there isn't even a medicine for them to take or for them to believe in? I remembered a book I'd read called "Remarkable Recovery" that told of many people who had recovered from diseases with terminal diagnoses. While there wasn't a single answer to how these people overcame their illnesses, there were striking similarities in their attitudes, beliefs, and characteristics. Some of these include:

- Accepting the diagnosis but rejecting the prognosis.

  ➢ Making decisions according to their particular belief systems and understandings, not someone else's.

  ➢ Having at least one special healing relationship and understanding with a loved one, a health professional, a friend, a support group, or a therapist.

81

➢ Getting in touch with unexpressed emotions.

➢ Rediscovering joy, creativity, a purpose in life, a sense of worth, a reason to be on this planet, or a feeling of fulfillment.

➢ The resolution and determination to transform their lives, careers, cities, or marriages.[1]

Many afternoons between therapy sessions, I sat in my wheelchair looking out the window, listening to an audio tape of Chicken Soup for the Soul[2]. The book was filled with stories of amazing people, such as that of Dr. Glenn Cunningham, who, as a child, recovered from burn injuries so severe that the doctors recommended amputating his legs. He refused the surgery and, through faith and determination, not only walked again but RAN. Dubbed "the Kansas Flyer," Glenn Cunningham ran the world's fastest mile in 1936. His favorite Bible verse was Isaiah 40:31:

But those who wait on the Lord shall renew their strength; they shall mount up with wings like eagles; they shall run and not be weary. They shall walk and not faint.[3]

Then there's the story of Morris Goodman who, while attempting to land his airplane one afternoon, crashed breaking his neck at C1-C2. The accident crushed his spinal cord and destroyed nearly every muscle in his body. Morris could no longer perform any bodily function except to blink his eyes. Doctors considered his injuries too severe to survive. But the man doctors later dubbed "The Miracle Man" did survive. And with a strong faith in God, courage, and determination, he not only rebuilt his body but also his mind and outlook on life.[4]

Once I read an article about Mother Maya, Sri Swamini Mayatitananda, one of the world's few female Vedic monks and a preeminent teacher of Ayurveda medicine. She said, "The main thing in life... is the cultivation of personal awareness of who we are—in charge of our purpose, in charge of our path...to help us understand that we have great medicine within our body, within our mind, within our constitution. Once we learn how to harness it, we can remain in the flow of healing." She added, "I do not see healing or the quantum leaps that the spirit can make as a miracle at all. It's quite the norm for us as humans."[5]

As I pondered the amazing stories of recovery that so many people had manifested in their lives, I wondered, what is the key to miracles? And what did Jesus really mean when he said,

Truly, truly, I say to you, the one who believes in me the works I do shall he do also, and greater than these shall he do, because I go to the Father? (John 14:12).

And

I say unto you, if ye have the faith as a grain of mustard seed, ye shall say unto this mountain, remove hence to yonder place; and it shall remove, and nothing shall be impossible unto you." (Matthew 17 19-21).

And finally,

When you make the two one [i.e., faith and emotion], you will become the sons of man, and when you say, 'Mountain move away,' it will move away. (Gospel of Thomas, #106, NHL).

By His words, Jesus meant that each and every one of us possesses the same potentiality as He to unite with the Holy Spirit and by so doing, are capable of transcending physical reality as typically understood by science. As Dr. Larry Dossey said in his book *Recovering the Soul*, "There is no great chasm separating man and God that temporal actions must bridge. The thing is to realize this interrelationship, not bring it into being or make it happen."[7]

The key to unlocking this potentiality is complete acceptance and letting go of preconceived ideas of what is possible in our lives and the universe. "*In other words, if you want to be healthy, you must stop thinking of yourself as sick. If you want to be prosperous and successful, you must renounce the practice of thinking of yourself as a failure.*"[8] As Paul said, *Be transformed by the renewal of your mind* (Roman 12:2). By releasing these biases, limitless possibilities are created. As Jesus said, through this divinity (also known as "The Kingdom of God"), *nothing shall be impossible to you.*[9]

It seemed to me that all miraculous healings, regardless of the technique employed, had three things in common:

1. **Clear intention.**
2. **Pray as though it is already done.**
3. **Take action to make it come to pass.**

As I pondered these things, certain words kept ringing in my ears: **faith, belief, desire, love, letting go of preconceptions, and determination**. One day prior to meditating, I asked God: Which of these words works the best? The response that came later was, "The one that works best for you."

Three times a week, we had group therapy. It was a nice change of pace that allowed me to interact with a variety of people. Our time together gave me the opportunity to meet some wonderful individuals: a man who had lost both of his legs in a car accident, several stroke victims, two people with spinal disease, and two gunshot victims. We were a diverse group but quickly bonded. And while everyone was apprehensive about their futures, we tried to put on a brave front.

Our little group of six would form a circle in the corner of the therapy room, where we performed various exercises disguised as games. In one game, a therapist tossed a balloon into the air above a patient, who was told to bat it to the person on their left, and so on. Although the game looked ridiculously simple, from the perspective of a wheelchair user with little ability to move, such games presented major challenges. The first time I played, I waited nervously as my turn approached. When the time came, the balloon seemed to float in slow motion toward me. Reaching out with one hand while gripping the chair with the other, I gave the balloon a whack. Slowly, it propelled in the general direction of the person on my left. Whew! My hit was far from perfect, but at least I kept from falling out of the wheelchair as I halfway expected to happen.

Watching others tap the balloon around the circle, I couldn't help but marvel at life's ironies. I'd seen many highs and lows in life, from being a morbidly shy youth to holding high-profile jobs with many responsibilities. It had been a wild ride. But this—sitting paralyzed in a wheelchair at age 51, lamely trying to bat a ten-cent balloon up into the air without embarrassing myself—had to be one of the classic scenes in the "movie of my life." The highs and lows, the advantages and disadvantages, and the good and bad of each person's life seemed meaningless. We were "one," united by a common bond of need and understanding. Whatever vanity I may have had, or sense of separateness from others regardless of the reason, was washed away in a tidal wave of love and understanding.

Occasionally I met with Dr. Patrick, a therapist who had suffered a similar injury to mine 20 years ago. Dr. Patrick had recovered enough from his injury to be able to walk but was still impaired. He stopped by once or twice a week after lunch to share his perspective on life as a spinal injury patient and to help me prepare for my now-disabled life. He shared many experiences and his advice was always practical, valuable, and heartfelt.

One in particular sticks in my mind. Shortly after Dr. Patrick's injury, when he was hospitalized and immobile, his nose began to itch. He tried not to think about it, but the more he tried, the worse the itch became. Finally, out of desperation, he asked a nun, an employee of the hospital who was visiting the next bed, whether she would scratch his nose for him. "No," she said indignantly. "How dare you be so selfish as to want your nose scratched when there are so many other patients here with more serious problems for me to attend to," and walked away in a huff. Dr. Patrick was left to suffer the agony of an itching nose, embarrassed with no way to scratch it. My heart went out to him. How frustrating and degrading to be at the mercy of people who are callous and condescending. In the time it took the nun to degrade and embarrass the helpless young man, she probably could have scratched the noses of everyone on the ward.

A week or so later, I had a somewhat similar experience. I had been exceptionally thirsty one night, a medication side effect, and requested my water cup to be refilled several times over the course of the evening. When I made the request the third or fourth time, the floor supervisor got on the intercom and said sternly, "Mr. McCord, we can't continually be bringing you water. You'll have to make do till morning."

Hearing this, I exploded. "I'm not a prisoner in this place and will request as much water as I need. I'm going to discuss this with the staff doctor in the morning." Shortly after, a full cup of water was brought.

Dr. Patrick's story and my experience reminded me that every encounter we have with another person is an opportunity to build them up or tear them down, to either reflect our love and appreciation of the Christ nature within them or to drive them further from understanding this Truth.

Occasionally, I met with Pat, the staff psychologist, to learn more about living with a spinal injury. I watched grim videos of people with seriously debilitating spinal injuries who had learned to live within their limitations. While painful to watch, they demonstrated the resilience of the human spirit.

These meetings also gave me a chance to interact with other spinal injury patients. One man had been a paraplegic 18 months earlier and worked his way back to mobility. Sadly, his condition had begun to deteriorate, and for the second time, he was back in a wheelchair facing an uncertain future. His brow furrowed with worry and fear showed in his eyes as he spoke to me. Helplessly, I listened to him lament about this cruel and unfair world. After that day, our universes spun in separate directions, and I never saw this man again or learned how things turned out for him. Whenever I think of him, I am reminded never to take any of life's blessings for granted and to appreciate every moment.

One Saturday afternoon, I received a surprise visit from Jared, the boy I had been mentoring through the "Youth Friends" program for several years. He came with his mother Marlene and another woman named Mary, the counselor at Jared's school. What a wonderful surprise! Seeing them, I felt connected to the real world for the first time in weeks.

Other times, Nancy or Gloria (associate ministers from Unity Church of Overland Park) visited. Even my barber Tony came to the hospital to give me a haircut. These visitations brightened an otherwise gloomy existence in the rehab hospital, particularly on weekends when the halls were mostly silent.

One night after dinner, as I sat in my wheelchair gazing out at the setting sun, I reflected upon the people who had visited or expressed their concerns during my stay at the rehab institute and how their actions had taken me by surprise. Then, my thoughts turned to my inner self. Who was I—really? Regardless of my accomplishments in life, such as they were, I was still plagued by the same sense of aloneness and self-doubt that had haunted me for years. It came to me that my way of thinking was in many ways similar to the words of the Simon and Garfunkel song "I Am a Rock," some of which go as follows:

I am shielded in my armor,
Hiding in my room, safe within my womb.
I touch no one and no one touches me.
I am a rock, I am an island.
And a rock feels no pain;
And an island never cries.[10]

Just as in the song, the wall I built around myself was "deep and mighty." But now, for the first time in my life, that wall was starting to crumble—not from a hammer but from the love of others. In particular, the flowers, thoughts, and prayers from fellow workers and classmates in a class I'd been taking at Unity moved me deeply. The next time Cindy came to visit, I dictated the following letter to her, which she wrote:

"For much of my life, my beliefs reflected the words of the song, 'Hiding in my room, safe within my womb, I touch no one, and no one touches me.' But now I see how wrong I've been. You have shown me how much we need one another, and that sometimes our smallest acts of kindness can have an effect upon others in ways we may never imagine. Because of your love and concern, I am committing myself for the rest of my life to doing what I can to help people in need, particularly those with spinal cord injuries."

I asked Cindy if she would deliver the letter to Jane's class and read it aloud to them. She delivered the letter but asked the teacher to read the letter to the class. I hope they understood my meaning.

Over time, several members of the staff—especially the nurse's aides—became good friends. My admiration grew for these angels of mercy who performed thankless tasks to ease the plights of others for modest pay, benefits, and little job security.

One day, Jarie came into my room. She'd been gone a few days, so I teasingly said to her, "Hey Jarie, where ya been hidin' yerself?"

"Oh," she sighed heavily, "I been in jail a few days. A while back, I got some traffic tickets over'n Overland Park. I ain't been there since, but last weekend, I had to go see 'bout gettin' my car fixed. Well, some policeman stopped me and when he found out about them traffic tickets, he done put me in jail. I'm out now, but what'm I gonna do? I ain't got the money to pay for those tickets or fix my car. And if I don't have a car, how'm I gonna get ta work ta make enough money to pay 'em? They'll send me back to jail for sure." "What'm I gonna do?" she kept repeating, eyes downcast, tears welling.

I patted her hand and tried to comfort her. I told her everything would work out. But neither of us could imagine how things would turn out. Slowly Jarie walked out of the room, shoulders drooping. I only saw her one other time. After that, she disappeared from my life forever and I never knew what happened.

On another occasion, I became embroiled in a dispute between a nurse's aide and her supervisor. The aide was a temporary hire who had just been fired. Before leaving, she tearfully told me that her supervisor falsely claimed that I had requested a shower but she had refused to give me one. "What am I going to do?" she said tearfully. "My husband is disabled and we need the money from this job." The supervisor's story was untrue. The next day, I asked for the head of the nursing department and told her the truth. The aide was soon reinstated and the lying supervisor terminated. It's funny how my presence, immobile as it was, had affected the lives of two people.

These experiences reminded me that everyone has problems in life, even if we can't see them, and that the decisions we make for ourselves and others have consequences that may last a lifetime. How much simpler it would be for us if we simply did what we knew to be right in the first place.

One week slowly blended into another, but I remained faithful to the message: Do what's doable whenever you can. Work on your areas of strength first. Don't give up.

Every day after therapy, whether in bed or in my wheelchair, I tried to do something even if it was simply wiggling a foot or moving my fingers. After a while, some therapists began calling me "24-7."

Eventually, I graduated from a large wheelchair to a smaller, more mobile version and became good at wheeling down the hallways. I took pride in zooming past slower-moving wheelchairs, grinning smugly without looking back to rub it in.

Occasionally, I watched incredulously as some patients argued or became angry when asked to do challenging and painful exercises. Once, a woman fell on the floor crying when her therapist instructed her to do a workout. Others did their work half-heartedly at best. A young man (whom I'll call Gene) had been in an auto accident and suffered a head injury. Although seriously injured, he was progressing and I'd seen him walking several times. One day, as we sat in the patient's lounge waiting for lunch, I asked Gene casually, "So, how long do you think it's going to be before you're walking normally again?" "Oh, I don't think I'm going to try to walk anymore," he said. "It's just too dangerous. I might fall." I said nothing but thought to myself, Are you nuts? Do you want to be like this for the rest of your life?

Several weeks later, I overheard Gene talking to one of the counselors. They were discussing options for nursing homes where he could go to live. Not long after that, he was gone to a nursing home, I assume. I imagine he's there to this day.

Each of us has a choice to make every moment of our lives meaningful, and only as individuals know the right thing to do. My wish is that people such as Gene would choose hope over fear.

I knew him only as Steen. He was a lovely African American man with a broad smile revealing a gap between his two front teeth. No matter, his smile lit up a room. Steen was completely dedicated to doing everything he could as a nurse's aide to make life for the patients under his care as comfortable as possible. Steen worked harder than any aide in the hospital and, because of his kindness, was sometimes taken advantage of by patients and other aides. He knew he was being taken advantage of, but it didn't matter to him. The only important thing for him was that his patients received the best possible care. He was devoutly religious, and many of his beliefs were more conservative or traditional than mine. No matter. The love he held in his heart for others had no bounds.

As a true Christian soldier, when Steen wasn't walking the halls of the Rehab Institute looking for a way to help people, he frequently walked some of the harshest ghettos of Kansas City and other cities far into the night. His mission was to hand out leaflets encouraging people to accept Jesus Christ as their Lord and Savior. Steen visited areas many would consider unsafe, but he wasn't concerned. What mattered was spreading the Word of God to people in need of hope.

I greatly admired Steen. Oftentimes, we had long conversations regarding faith, religion, and life. Although we came from vastly different backgrounds, both personal and spiritual, we shared a belief in the power of prayer (my belief being relatively new) and an understanding that love for our fellow man is the key to the world's future.

Steen was terribly shy when it came to women and had never married. One day, he told me he knew a woman named Gloria, whom he admired and was friends with. Gloria was also single and active in the same church. He had a secret crush on her but was too shy to ask her out. Gamely, I tried to build Steen's confidence by reminding him of his many good attributes and suggested ways he could ask her out. But it was hopeless. He was too unsure of himself and never asked Gloria for a date. Later, Gloria met another man with whom she began a relationship, and Steen became remorseful.

We maintained contact for a while after Steen left the Institute but eventually lost touch. Years later, I tried to track him down but he had disappeared. I hope he is doing well and was finally able to find the love of another human, which he so richly deserved. If I could speak to him today, I would ask him to accept his perfection and follow his heart's desire now rather than wait for tomorrow.

Once a week, all the seriously impaired patients got together to fix a lunch we had voted upon the week before. Not only was it an opportunity to develop the life skills that most would need after we left the Rehab Institute, but it also was a time to forget our problems, laugh, and simply be together for a while. Regardless of our differences, the same inner beauty and innocence shined from each person's eyes. Just as with Steen, each person was perfect in their own unique way. We reveled in each other's joys and agonized in each person's setbacks.

Even in my isolated bubble of a world, I couldn't escape the drama of human events taking place in the surrounding environment. Every night, the screams of police and emergency vehicle sirens filled my room as they rushed to the scene of some accident or catastrophe. They often pulled into the emergency entrance of Trinity Hospital directly across the street, their emergency lights casting crazily shaped, rapidly whirling shadows across my walls and ceiling.

Other times, I watched a real-life silent movie unfold before my eyes at the entrance to that hospital from the window of my room on the second floor. Once, I saw a man wave goodbye to a woman. Another time, a child blew a kiss to his mom. Every day, a steady stream of people came and went from the hospital or sat at the small rest area outside the building, enjoying a moment of peace. One overcast afternoon, two policemen escorted a young woman out of the hospital. Suddenly, she jerked away from them and began screaming and crying. In the ensuing struggle, she fell to the ground. The police officers wrestled control of her, pushed her roughly into a squad car, and then sped away. Life was going on with all its wonders, warts, and worries.

A simple idea popped into my head: Every action at its basic level originates from love or a cry for love. What a different world it would be if everyone understood this truth. We could eliminate judgment, hatred, and fear—the causes of strife and war—not only between people but among nations.

I assumed life was hard for Cindy while I was gone. She actively managed her job, household, and unexpected crises, like the day when the dishwasher broke, spewing hundreds of gallons onto the faux wood kitchen floor. The floor was ruined; she had to file an insurance claim. There were many additional responsibilities, but she seemed to handle it well. I think she enjoyed being in control. One day, she brought several floor designs for the kitchen, and we chose the one we liked best. Ironically, working together to resolve the floor crisis was the single most bonding experience we shared during my time in the hospital. However, except for Friday nights, she didn't come to the hospital much, and I only saw Sean or Ryan once during my time at the Rehab Institute. While I desperately wanted to see them more, I had insisted they not change their lives because of me.

From time to time I talked to Megan, the Institute's family counselor. I told Megan about the long-standing difficulties in my marriage in the hope that she could do something to help the situation. To my delight, she agreed to talk to Cindy then bring us together to talk about our difficult issues. Our interests had diverged, but perhaps we could find a way to meet each other halfway.

For days, I waited anxiously to learn the results of Megan's meeting with Cindy. Finally the results were in and they were not as I had hoped. Megan told me how much happier Cindy was without me in her life. She felt better not having to follow what I thought were mutually agreed-upon household rules. Until that moment, I'd not fully understood the depth of Cindy's unhappiness and resentment toward me. Even worse, Megan informed me that she was still in school and had not yet been certified to be a counselor. In other words, she had been lying to me for 18 months.

Because of this, Megan said she didn't feel qualified to bring Cindy and me together for a joint counseling session after all. The scab that had overlaid our difficulties for so many years had been pulled off without any medication to heal the wound. I resented Megan for her lack of professionalism and the damage she had caused. For the first time since the injury, I cried.

One day, I met a freckled teenager about 17 years old being wheeled toward the therapy room in a large wheelchair similar to the one I'd used for many weeks. I sensed his spinal injury was similar to mine. As our eyes locked, I smiled and gave him a thumbs-up. It wasn't to be the last of our encounters.

As the weeks passed, I became able to walk farther and farther. With Randy maintaining a firm grip on my safety belt, I went from walking around the gym to doing the entire perimeter inside the building. Other times, I practiced going up and down stairs. The decline, in particular, terrified me. But each time I succeeded, my confidence grew.

To my surprise, one sunny spring day, Randy casually said, "Let's go outside." Except for the few times I wheeled out the front door to sit under the cupola to enjoy the evening air, I hadn't experienced the outside world for over two months. With another therapist pushing my wheelchair, Randy directed me to walk down the sidewalk. Oh, what a sensation! The gentle breeze, exquisitely green grass just starting to peak from the soil, the song of a lone bird in a nearby tree, and the fantastically shaped clouds floating high above me, not framed by a window. Plodding happily along like an obedient puppy with Randy holding the leash, I reveled in the sights and sounds of the great outdoors. But the thrill only lasted a short while as after about 200 feet, I collapsed in exhaustion into my wheelchair.

The next day, we took another outdoor walk. This time, I made it to an alley and back to the front of the Institute, a distance of about 400 feet. Although it was a chilly March day, the sensation of cold on my skin had never felt so exhilarating! The thrill of experiencing the "real world" from an upright position rather than from a stretcher or wheelchair intoxicated my senses with the euphoria I'd almost forgotten.

Finally, the big day came: the day of my release from the Institute. While I still spent most of my time in a wheelchair, I could walk reasonably well with the aid of a walker. The day before, I'd been tested and found to have eight percent of the strength of an average adult my age on my left side.

My left side felt about ten pounds heavier than the right side, and I still had to use a catheter to urinate. I'd regained many sensations throughout my body, even though they varied from area to area and weren't nearly as acute as before the injury. Whenever I shifted my position or stood up, I experienced muscle spasms lasting up to a minute, which made my entire body quiver like a leaf rustling in the wind. And while I could use my hands reasonably well, I had difficulty holding eating utensils properly or performing seemingly small tasks. Every task was a challenge, every success a victory. Many factors affected my mobility and dexterity, including air temperature, how much sleep I'd gotten the night before, and my attitude. I still wore a neck collar and would continue to do so for another two months. Each night was an adventure in pain that many times left me screaming in agony. I looked forward to dawn's first light because it meant I had survived another tortuous night. But none of this mattered. I was going home!

At the last session with my occupational therapist, Cathy, she told me as gently as possible that I probably would have limited use of my left hand for the rest of my life. During my last session with Randy, he was unusually quiet. We sat alone in silence for a long while in the gym that I'd grown to know so well. Finally, he said, "Mike, I can finally tell you some things I've been wanting to tell you for a long time now. Only about 10 percent of people with your kind of spinal injury ever walk again. In my career, I've never had a patient who couldn't initially sit up or walk again. What you've done is amazing, but I want you to know you're always going to have some impairments, so try to get used to it. Please don't try to do more than you're capable of doing, such as the mountain climbing thing."

Silently, I studied Randy's face. Until that moment, I had never fully realized the severity of my injury. I knew Randy had my best interests at heart and didn't want me to be let down by having too high expectations. However, I simply couldn't understand why he didn't feel I could go farther—that I should be satisfied with what I'd achieved and let it go at that.

When I got back to my room, I looked one more time at my "road map to recovery" that, by now, I knew so very well:

Do what's doable whenever you can. Work on your areas of strength first, and never give up.

Slowly, I peeled the paper off the wall. Although the words were extremely meaningful to me, I knew someone who needed them more now. Piece of paper in hand, I slowly wheeled myself down the hall to Eric's room, the freckle-faced teenager who had an injury similar to mine. With him watching from his bed, his mother at his side, I gave the paper to his father and told him how the message had come to me in the intensive care unit at the hospital.

"This message is vital to me," I said, "but now it's even more important to your son. Please take it." Eric's father looked deeply into my eyes as tears welled in his. As I was leaving the room, he handed it to Eric.

After saying goodbye to the many friends I'd made over the past several weeks, I returned to the room that had been my universe.

As the 1:00 p.m. release time approached, I put my few belongings into a duffel bag, turned the wheelchair toward the doorway, and sat anxiously staring at the elevator in the hallway, anticipating the moment when it would open and Cindy would step out to take me home. However, 1:00 p.m. came and went, as did 2:00, then 3:00.

As time wore on, I became increasingly worried that something might have happened to her. The delay allowed me to reflect on the truths revealed during my time at the rehab institute—truths I had previously overlooked or not fully comprehended. I saw the faces of those who impacted my life profoundly and blessed them. My eyes opened significantly more than before the accident. Can I apply these truths in the everyday world outside the hospital? Time will tell. Sometimes, knowing and doing are two different things. What about Cindy and me? Could the fissures in our relationship be healed, or was it too late?

Finally, around 3:15 p.m., Cindy stepped out of the elevator, five hours late. While greatly relieved she was OK, there was no explanation for the delay. Perhaps she wanted to send a message to let me know that she was in control now. Or maybe there was something else. For the moment, it didn't matter. I was going home.

Chapter 12
Picking up the Pieces

With senses filled to overflowing by the sights and sounds of the world whizzing by during the drive home, we made small talk: "How is school going for the boys?" "How are things at your job, Cindy?" The pleasant chatter carefully avoided several elephants in the room, such as how my physical disabilities were going to affect our lifestyles and the future of our relationship.

Thirty minutes later, the car turned the last corner and our house came into view for the first time in eight weeks. The car pulled into the drive and slowed to a stop. Gingerly opening the car door, I set my walker outside and pulled myself out of the car. After the muscle spasm from head to foot ended, I firmly grasped the bars on the walker, smiled at the beautiful sight of "home," and slowly began trudging toward the house as its poles clanged and wheels crunched noisily on the concrete below. At the porch, I grimaced in anticipation of the effort it would take to raise each of my legs above the three-stepped porch. Upon reaching the landing, Cindy held the door open, and I entered the living room I'd last seen lying face down at floor level weeks ago.

Everything was terrific and alive! The plants, the colors, the décor, the soft chairs. Taka and Sabrina were happy to see me in their "cat" way, but Darby was overjoyed, bathing my face in kisses with his wet tongue, his bugged eyes shining brightly with happiness. Of course, Sean and Ryan were also happy to see me. I was overjoyed to be back home with them.

There wasn't a special celebration, dinner, or much of anything else to distinguish that day from any other. After getting caught up in my sons' life events, they left to do other things. My conversations with Cindy were pleasant but began to lag after we'd finished discussing the day's significant events. Life went on as usual after the initial hubbub of the welcome home. Perhaps much of their attitude was a reflection of my own, which was not to look at my situation as permanent. Nonetheless, I couldn't shake the feeling that my homecoming was kind of an intrusion on their lives. Whether real or imagined, it was clear my life was in pieces. Putting it back together again was going to be a Herculean task.

Fortunately, our house had a kitchen and a bath on two levels, one of which was on the lower level. This level had a sitting room with a TV and a computer room. The Rehab Institute had recommended making the house handicap accessible, which Cindy had arranged to have completed. The Institute also placed a hospital bed in the sitting room. Although my mobility was limited, I could get from my bed to my wheelchair and later to a walker to go into the adjoining kitchen and bathroom. I could walk out onto a covered patio overlooking our serene backyard with beautiful hardwood trees and an orchard. Although restrictive, it was a comfortable arrangement. I savored sitting on the deck, drinking in the sights and sounds of nature for hours on end. Because I couldn't get up the stairs, this area of the house became my world for the next three months.

When nighttime came, nature's bliss was replaced by cold reality in the form of freezing temperatures. The temperature dropped to around 20 degrees as the wind howled. The storm doors to the patio had never been properly sealed, resulting in a steady draft when the wind blew. This lower level of the house became much colder than the rest. After watching TV with me till around 9 p.m., Cindy and Ryan went upstairs to do other things. Eventually, the house became quiet and I knew they'd gone to bed. It was OK, as I was used to being alone in the quiet. After a while, I shut off the TV and bedside light and tried to go to sleep. However, the room temperature continued to fall, enhanced by wind whistling beneath the patio doors. I pulled the only light blanket tightly around my neck, then over my head, but the chill seeped underneath in spite of my dulled sensations. As the rest of the household slept two floors above, my icebox on the ground floor became a nightmare, an ordeal never to be forgotten.

During the ensuing days, reality set in: while I could do more for myself than a few weeks earlier, I still depended heavily upon others' assistance. Cindy did countless thankless tasks for me, such as bringing food, medicine, clean clothes, washing my laundry, unscrewing the lids of bottles, and taking me to doctor appointments. She also rented videos for us to watch. However, there was simply no getting around the fact that caring for me was a weighty burden, and I hated to ask. The strain soon began to show in her demeanor. She had become accustomed to my not being around, and before long, it became evident that my return was an annoyance; little things would set her off.

Cindy bought a small refrigerator and placed it in my lower-level kitchen. It was a handy way to store cold food that I could not get by myself. After dinner, one week to the day of my coming home, Ryan placed a bottle of juice sideways in the small refrigerator just before he and Cindy went upstairs for the evening. A few minutes later, I struggled out of bed, took hold of my walker, and began shuffling into the kitchen. Rounding the kitchen corner, I saw a growing puddle of liquid from the refrigerator that looked like fruit juice streaming across the floor. Leaving my walker, I hobbled toward the refrigerator, opened the door, and leaned down to set the juice upright. Suddenly, my weak right leg gave out, and I crumpled to the floor in a heap on top of the leg in an awkward position. A sharp pain shot up my leg. Unable to get up, I lay helplessly on the floor.

Summoning my voice, I yelled for help. A few minutes later, Cindy came rushing downstairs with Ryan behind her. But when she saw me lying on the floor with my leg still underneath me, to my surprise, she exploded into a rage, cursing me in a continuous flow as Ryan stood watching silently in the doorway. With rising anger, she picked up anything she could get her hands on and began throwing them at me. Feebly, I tried to dodge the flying projectiles. "You stupid son of a bitch! Why weren't you watching what you're doing? I'm so sick of you." It was too much for Ryan, and he ran up the stairs. After finishing her tirade, she also went upstairs, leaving me alone on the floor.

After collecting my senses, I began crawling through the wet floor toward the wheelchair in the other room near the door, covering myself in juice in the process. Upon reaching it, I tried to hold it steady and pull myself into the seat, but my hand slipped, and the chair rolled away. Wearily, my kitten-strength body settled onto the cool floor as the pain increased. Suddenly, Cindy reappeared at the doorway and gave the wheelchair a push toward me. She must have been standing halfway up the stairs. She said nothing but held the chair steady to make it easier for me to get in. But I was also angry by now and told her to leave—"I'll do it myself!" She left. Finally, pulling myself into the chair, I wheeled to my bed, struggling back into it. The remainder of the night was sleepless and painful. Alone in the dark, I wondered why she had been so angry: the culmination of a lifetime of frustration from living with me? The disappointment of my having yet another accident? Or was it something else? I'll never know because we never again spoke of the events that night.

At dawn's first light, I struggled out of bed into the wheelchair and rolled over to the stairway. Cautiously grabbing the stair handrails, I tried to stand up. The pain was excruciating. Slumping to my knees, I took each stair step a knee at a time. Slowly, the kitchen floor came into view. Once in the kitchen, I crawled across the floor to the landline phone. With great effort and several false starts, I got the phone off the hook and called Nebraska. Hearing my mother's voice on the other end was a heavenly balm. I told her what had been happening and that I feared for my safety. Mom said the first thing I needed to do was get to a hospital as soon as possible. She also said Dad and my brother would be in Olathe within 48 hours.

When Cindy awoke, I asked her to call the emergency room and take me there because I knew something was wrong. She did so, and in a short time we were at an all too familiar place—the same hospital where the ambulance had taken me the night I broke my neck. X-rays revealed a fractured tibia just above the right ankle. "We don't want you doing this anymore," the on-duty doctor looming above me lectured condescendingly. In dead silence, we waited for a cast to be fitted onto my leg. Looking back on what happened that black night, I think Cindy's reaction was motivated by fear and frustration because of all the stress she'd been under since the initial injury and all the trouble I'd caused.

The doctors said the leg would take four to six weeks to heal. The optimism I'd felt since getting out of the hospital was replaced by despair. For days I stared numbly out the patio doors in sullen silence. What have I ever done to deserve such horrible things? Am I that bad of a person? There was no answer.

As might be expected, Sean and Ryan were upset at this latest turn of events, but we never had a meaningful conversation on the subject. While I wished they were more involved with my recovery efforts, I accepted it for what it was. They had a lot of issues to deal with in their own lives, and I didn't want them to feel obligated. It took a few days, but I eventually viewed the latest turn of events as just another flawed, temporary curve in the road that would not affect my long-term prospects for recovery. I'd always been taught to "suck it up" when times get tough. Expecting help simply wasn't the way my family looked at things. Still, I hurt inside.

The following Monday, Dad and my brother Rod arrived. They came during the day when I was home alone. Seeing them was as though the cavalry had arrived to save me! Rod rigged a phone in the basement so I could call out in an emergency. Soon thereafter, Rod left on the four-and-a-half-hour return trip to Nebraska. However, Dad stayed the following week. His presence calmed the household. He made it clear to Cindy that a reoccurrence of "that" night had better not ever happen again! My care improved.

The following Monday, a handicapped-person bus stopped in front of the house to take me 20 miles to the Rehabilitation Institute where I would begin outpatient day therapy. What a sight I must have made toddling down the driveway behind a walker, one leg in a cast and wearing a neck brace. The driver must have thought I'd been in a train wreck which, in a sense, was true. Three times a week for the next month, I repeated the drill: carefully maneuvering myself onto the front porch, gingerly descending each step to the sidewalk, and then embarking on the tedious trek down our long driveway to the waiting bus. While getting there was difficult, the additional therapy was a godsend. It enabled me to continue working with professionals to improve strength, flexibility, and dexterity.

Two weeks later, I was working out on a stationary bike in the gym when I saw Eric, the young man to whom I'd given my "roadmap to recovery." He was walking with a therapist at his side and never noticed me as he strode by with a confident look and only a slight limp. No matter. I smiled inwardly, knowing he was well on the road to recovery.

During the bus ride to therapy one day, a paraplegic man about 40 years old got on. He held several oil paintings under his arm, so I asked him about them. He told me his career had been ruined 20 years ago when he was paralyzed as a result of an auto accident. Unable to do the work he'd done previously, he decided to try to develop his artistic skills, which until then had been a hobby. In rehab, he began taking painting classes. In time, with practice and patience, he enhanced his artistic abilities so much that he embarked upon a much more lucrative profession selling landscape paintings throughout the United States. He was excited because his annual "Art in the Woods" exhibit was fast approaching. His tenacity and optimism were infectious, his perseverance inspiring.

A few weeks after my ankle incident, I resumed seeing Jared, my "lunch buddy" through the "Youth Friends" Program. Unable to drive, I was picked up by Mary, the school counselor. She drove to Burger King where I bought two lunches that included a toy Jared liked, then to school where we would share our lunches and talk. Jared was an extremely intelligent boy. With proper guidance, he had a bright future. Mary took me home after our lunch. Her willingness to go the extra mile meant a great deal to both Jared and me. Months later, I was surprised to learn I had been selected "Youth Friend of the Year" by the Olathe School District. Truly, Mary deserved the award for going above and beyond the call of duty by picking me up and taking me home. She was a model of the dedication of all educators in this country.

On the days I didn't have therapy, I'd forget my cares and sit on the back patio for hours, sipping tea and absorbing the simple magnificence of nature in springtime. The sun never felt so delicious on my face or the gentle breeze on my skin. From above, birds sang as they flitted from one majestic branch to another on the wise old pin oak tree that grew near the patio. Bright leaves bursting from graceful limbs shimmered in golden sunlight swaying in the wind. The air was never so clean, the sky never so blue, or the cotton candy clouds never so impossibly white. Even the gentle buzz of flies as they flitted about was as melodious as a Mozart symphony. Through eyes with as much wonderment as those of a child, I saw sunbeams form intricate patterns on the bark of a nearby white ash tree. The universe was new to me, one that was filled with miracles and love. Over and over, I gave thanks for a second chance to experience these moments of God's creation. And as one moment was replaced by the next, I also gave thanks for that moment as well.

That spring was a good month. My leg had healed and the cast was removed. Finally, I could discard the neck cast I'd worn continuously for the past four months. My spirits received an added boost when, in the third week of May, I began working from home on a limited basis. The bank generously adapted my home computer to connect with their systems and even sent my supervisor from Chicago to help set it all up for me. My brain felt sluggish and unfocused, but it felt good to contribute to society again, even in a small way.

Before I could go back to the office, I needed to be able to drive again, legally. Fortunately, the Rehab Institute gave driving tests. One day, toward the end of my time as an outpatient, I took the eye exam, dexterity exam, and written exam, followed by a driving test. I was as nervous as a sophomore in high school. When I learned I'd passed the driving test, I felt the same joy I had when passing it as a 16-year-old.

Being able to drive again was a huge victory in my challenge to live a normal life again. Just knowing I had the freedom to leave the house whenever I wanted was a massive boost to my badly damaged self-esteem. It also marked the return of another of those blessings in life that most of us take for granted. However, once that freedom is taken away, walls quickly grow around one's world, restricting it in ways that subtly but methodically destroy both will and confidence. The feeling that came with the knocking down of those walls was exhilarating. I vowed never again to take anything in life for granted.

From simple things such as managing my body functions, dressing myself, or fixing a cup of coffee to my material lot in life, whatever it may be, I gave eternal thanks. The unimportance of ego attachment to self, money, and material possessions became ever more apparent.

Toward the end of May, I began driving my car to the bus stop to catch the commuter bus from Olathe for the 45-minute drive to my office in downtown Kansas City. By now, I had graduated from the wheelchair to a walker most of the time, which ironically made it more difficult to maneuver while carrying my briefcase. Once off the bus, there was the arduous three-quarter block journey to my office in the city's largest skyscraper. Some other pedestrians looked at me with sympathy, others were oblivious, and some were annoyed that I might get in their way. But I was ecstatic! Being able to go to work again was exciting. Now that's an absolute miracle! Having to work and maintain a daily schedule also helped restore some of my lost confidence and self-esteem.

The flip side was that after residing in a quiet, solitary, and timeless world for many months, the "real" world seemed like a madhouse. I knew I would eventually get used to all the craziness, but something more disturbing was becoming increasingly apparent. My brain seemed to have gone mushy through the months of inactivity. Although I tried to concentrate, it was not easy to regain my mental sharpness. While living in a netherworld of meditation and quiet reflection was a blissful utopia, it didn't pay the bills. Although rebelling at the thought, I inevitably knew that some of the sublime beauty that engulfed my senses had to be tempered in order to function in the everyday world. However, making the shift was difficult. If my mind had slipped so much in just a few months, I could only imagine how hard it must be for people who are unable to participate in society for long periods of time. It gave me a new appreciation of their courage and strength.

April's showers turned to May's flowers. I settled into a new but peculiar routine. Since my father's visit, Cindy took care of my every need and things became better between us, at least on the surface. My mood varied from day to day; at times, I wasn't an easy person to live with. Although I could walk on a limited basis with a cane and my hand dexterity was continuing to improve, I suffered a lot of pain and frustration at not being able to do things as easily as in the past. Some days, the world seemed filled with promise, while others filled with despair. Sadly, at times, I lost sight of the important message I'd been given to live in a world of love rather than fear.

By the end of May, I had completely discarded the use of the wheelchair in favor of a walker and, at times, a cane. This was a big milestone! The walker made quite a racket and what a sight I must have made for the neighbors as I toddled down the street for a block or two on my daily walk. Meanwhile, the old cane that had so mysteriously appeared on the front seat of my Mustang twenty-one years earlier became important. The long-forgotten relic was now playing an essential role in my recovery. Was it a coincidence or part of a divine plan?

The annual Kansas City Highland Festival was held the second week of June. For years, I had sponsored a booth for Clan McCord. Although there were a lot of physical challenges in setting up a booth, I decided to do so again. The two-day event celebrates all things Scottish and includes a tribute to Scottish clans known as *The March of the Clans*. I had been District Chieftain for my Clan for years because of the book I'd written about my family's history. I enjoyed the event because it was a weekend of escapism into a bygone era deeply ingrained within my heritage. Just a few short months earlier, I doubted ever again being able to experience this fantastical world.

Alone, I drove to the festival's location and, with difficulty, erected the tent and set out various memorabilia for my booth. As noon drew near, I hoisted the T-pole upon which a five-foot cloth banner of our Clan Heraldry was affixed. I then limped over to the parade grounds where representatives of over 20 clans from throughout the United States were gathering for the march. Silently praying not to fall down or somehow embarrass myself, I waited in line behind representatives of Clan Kerr. A trio of musicians in full Scottish regalia ceremoniously marched to the front of the procession and began playing "Scotland the Brave" on bagpipe and drum. The march began. With one hand, I held the Clan McCord banner as high in the air as I could while gripping my cane with the other hand. My banner depicts an Irish Demi-Savage holding a barbed arrow in his left hand and a heart in his right hand, while the motto read, "Via Una Cor Unam," meaning "One Heart, One Way."

Before a crowd of several hundred spectators, the tartan-clad procession with clan banners fluttering gently in the wind proceeded slowly around the arena to the skirl of bagpipes and the militaristic rat, tat, tat of drums. Each person proudly represented his family's clan heritage. Toward the end, I began limping heavily but was reinvigorated when I heard two people clapping. Glancing to my side, I saw Cindy and her friend smiling and clapping. Grinning sheepishly, I pushed onward. Lost in the moment's excitement was the fact that I'd achieved another goal on my path to recovery or that, once again, Sean or Ryan was not present.

My connection with the Rehab Institute continued past my time as a patient. With my best buddy Darby, we began visiting patients in the hospital through the Pet Pals program. Patients were crazy about my little Boston Terrier with his pug nose, bugged eyes, big ears, and stripe down the middle of his face. Although lively, Darby was always extremely gentle with the patients and let everyone pet him who cared to. He was an immediate sensation with all who met him while I was an afterthought! I did my best to give encouragement and a sense of hope to those who seemed to need it. The fact that not long ago, I'd been a patient just like them seemed to make an impact.

One day as Darby's toenails clicked on the vinyl floor beside me, we walked down the hallway during our weekly visit and came to a room filled with young people in their late teens or early 20s. The patient, a young man about 19, had been permanently paralyzed as a result of a construction accident. Although the accident happened recently, the young man was optimistic and in good spirits. "I don't care about this injury," he said, "I'm going to get a paralegal degree so I can have a good job." I admired his guts and "can do" attitude and told him so. As I told my story, the look of resolve in his eyes grew ever stronger.

Darby and I continued to visit the hospital throughout the summer until the inpatient section of the Rehabilitation Hospital was unexpectedly closed. What a blow! What were the patients to do? The Rehab Institute was the only place of its kind in the Kansas City area. I fretted: what's going to happen to all the poor people who don't have health insurance? There wasn't an answer. The loss of the crucial services that the Rehab Institute provided to bedridden people was yet another casualty of a profit-driven world.

After the inpatient portion of the Institute closed, I tried to get us involved in a similar type of program, but there was a problem. The new group required dogs to pass an obedience test before they were allowed to visit patients. One of the test requirements was for the dog to stay one minute after his master had walked away. No way! My devoted little Darby immediately followed me when I moved away from him. As a result, Darby flunked his test, and we could no longer visit hospital patients. Darby was so embarrassed! It was sad not only because I lost the opportunity to bring my message of hope to people who needed to hear it but also because the patients loved my sweet little Boston.

As the summer wore on, I took three more steps on the road to recovery--with an unexpected bonus. One day in late June, as I stood in front of the urinal trying to "go" on my own before finally giving up and catheterizing, I suddenly urinated naturally. Unless you've been in this situation, you have no idea what a big deal it is. Excitedly, I broke the big news to anyone and everyone who would listen, adding jokingly that I could have sworn I faintly heard the sound of people singing the Hallelujah Chorus when the "big event" took place. While everyone responded with a peculiar smile, their eyes said something like, "You sure are weird." They probably thought I'd lost my marbles over such a trivial detail of life or, just as likely, that it was far more information than they needed! But to me, it was another example of something we take for granted in life until it's taken from us.

The second milestone occurred on the Fourth of July when I walked a mile with the aid of my cane "from the fifth dimension," as I'd come to call it. While I limped slowly along one of my favorite old jogging routes, I watched puffy white clouds hanging lazily in the sky and taking on the shapes of both real and mythical creatures. Occasionally, the melodic song of a distant meadowlark wafted on the gentle breeze. Thank you, I whispered over and over again, for the privilege of being able to experience something I'd always taken for granted again. Subsequently, I walked every chance I got, going a bit further each time.

I began doing modest cardiovascular work to complement walking to increase my strength. I also used a hand resister to increase the strength of both my hands and fingers. Initially, I was weak as a kitten and could only lift a 2.5-pound weight with my arms and 20-pound resistance against my legs. But ever so slowly, the strength in my muscles began to increase. The day I graduated to a five-pound bar was the third milestone of the summer. Everyone in the house was excited, including Darby, of course! Darby was excited about nearly every event in life. With the accomplishment of each goal, however small, larger ones came to mind. I wonder if I will be able to walk ten miles by the end of the year, I asked myself. What an unexpected bonus that would be! No way, that's crazy talk, a part of me said. Or is it, the other part asked?

What a relief it was to have a steady paycheck again and not need to rely upon rapidly dwindling sick leave benefits. Ryan was preparing to enter his first year of college, so we faced heavy financial obligations. Fortunately, we had saved for our son's college education for years and could draw on the savings for major expenditures, but there were still many smaller out-of-pocket costs.

The summer before Ryan left for college, things seemed to ease between Cindy and me. Sometimes, we would go to the library and get movies or videos on such topics as alternative healing and the power of the mind. When we got home, Cindy fixed 7-Up and sherbet floats for both of us to enjoy while we watched a video, she in her chair and me in my hospital bed. The positive messages of the videos were motivational for both of us. At times like this, I'd look over at my wife, a woman I loved, and think: perhaps, just perhaps, it's not too late for us.

Chapter 13
The Long and Lonely Road

For over a year, troubling rumors about my employer's future had swirled. The company had gone through a major acquisition and consolidation the year before, and ominous talk of layoffs, office closings, and reorganization constantly buzzed around the water cooler. However, I held onto the belief that my job was secure because, even though a salary freeze had gone into effect, I was given an excellent stock option instead of a raise. I also received an award for my community service activities. Surely these gestures were an indication that the company was pleased with my work and that I was in their long-term plans.

Then, early in July, the other person in my department resigned. Ignoring the warning signs, I rationalized that one less employee in the department would only improve my chances of job stability. Wrong! Late on a Friday afternoon, my boss called from Chicago to inform me that my department and job were being eliminated. Stunned, I walked to my car in a daze, heading home for the day.

Upon arriving home, I gathered my strength, called the family together, and told them I'd been let go from my job. For what seemed the umpteenth time, we once again were going from financial stability to instability. Trying to put on a brave front, I reassured everyone that things would be okay because of the four-week severance package I'd been given. But secretly, there was no plan, and I was scared. Unable to eat the pizza I'd ordered for everyone, I got in the car and drove to a secluded country road to be alone. After parking the car, I began walking. Head down with eyes focused on the gravel in front of me, I shuffled down the road with questions repeating themselves continuously in my mind: What was going on in my life? First, the accident, and now this, four months later. What did I do to deserve this? Is the universe conspiring to defeat and destroy me? What does it mean? What am I going to do now, crippled and unemployed? Who would hire a person with my disabilities? The questions went unanswered. Eventually, I came to a bridge overlooking a small stream. The only sounds came from water gurgling over the moss-covered rocks far below. The ordinarily cheerful sound was mournful. Except for the water, everything was deadly quiet as though I were the last person on earth. I leaned heavily on the bridge railing, covered my eyes, and began to cry for only the second time since the accident. After a while, I looked back at the road, which now seemed to symbolize life's long, lonely journey. Finally, I gathered my strength, rose to my feet, and, limping worse than usual, began the long walk back to the car.

Friday, July 31, 2001, was my last day at work. Slowly, I packed my personal belongings and walked out of the office for the final time. Although I'd have a few weeks of severance salary, I knew it wouldn't last long. Then what? I had no idea. To the bank's credit, the CEO tried to help me find a job elsewhere, though he was unsuccessful.

I dreaded starting another job search but resigned myself to the struggle that lay ahead. However, a few days later, before I had really begun the search, something totally unexpected happened. A local private commercial real estate appraiser with whom I had worked at the bank called. Dan had heard the news and asked whether I would consider working with him. We'd split the fee on appraisals we worked on together. While working independently wasn't my first choice, I leaped at the opportunity to join an established firm even though Dan was pretty much a "one-man show." A few days later, we met for lunch and worked out the details. As an added bonus, Dan specialized in complex commercial appraisals, which would give me valuable experience. Excitedly, I shared the news with Cindy, her face softening with relief.

Before long, I was working on complex commercial assignments. While the pay wasn't much, it was better than nothing. Additionally, as I learned long ago, never turn your back on an opportunity because oftentimes one door opening leads to other opportunities. Most importantly, it reminded me that angels come in many guises.

One morning several weeks later, as I was struggling to understand Dan's way of doing things, I received a call from Randy, my physical therapist. He and Cathy, my occupational therapy specialist, were preparing to speak to the therapy students at Rockhurst University in Kansas City, Missouri, and wanted to know whether I'd be willing to say a few words about my accident. Nervously, I agreed.

When I arrived at the lecture hall the following Tuesday, about 100 students and faculty were sitting in the gym. Randy introduced me by giving a medical description of my injury and diagnosis. I had long since memorized the ugly statistics:

- Neck-break between the C5 and C6 vertebrae,
- Low-functioning Class C quadriplegic
- Couldn't sit up initially.

I felt myself blush as Randy described my condition when I was first admitted to the Rehab Institute. He spoke of the trials, tribulations, successes, and failures that we'd gone through together and repeated what was common knowledge within the therapy profession: that most people with my type of injury never walk again. He said I'd overcome the odds due to hard work and determination. Then came my time to speak. After expressing my gratitude to Randy, Cathy, and everyone else at the Institute, I spoke of my belief in the power of the mind, the truth of the mind-body connection, and the power of faith.

As I told the story of my participation in the "March of the Clans" at the Scottish Highland Festival, I saw something I had never seen before. Randy was wiping a tear from his eye. In all our time together, this was the only time he had ever shown any emotion. After I finished, Randy addressed the audience and said, "Mike's story reminds me why I decided to become a physical therapist."

Afterward, students came up and shook my hand and echoed Randy's feelings. A lady stopped me in the hallway on my way to the car. Introducing herself as the Dean of the Therapy Department at Rockhurst University, she said that, as a result of my message, she'd decided to add more courses to the therapy curriculum emphasizing the importance of the mind-body connection. I watched in silence as she walked down the hall, her heels echoing loudly before disappearing around the corner. Had all this happened for reasons such as this? Could my injury be meant to serve a larger purpose: to spread an important message of hope to others facing severe life challenges? And, if so, was I capable of adequately expressing the message? I still ask myself those questions.

As August came to an end, Ryan left for college at Kansas State University in Manhattan. The day he left was a sad one because it meant that both our boys were gone. Although it was the beginning of an exciting new adventure in Ryan's life, it was the end of a significant one in ours.

Once Ryan was gone, things quickly went downhill between Cindy and me. The days of watching movies together ended abruptly, and she became increasingly absent from home. Her girlfriend Judy owned a shop at the mall where Cindy volunteered. Judy and the shop became primary in her life. Before long, they were taking trips together to faraway places to buy merchandise for the shop. I felt the former thread of Cindy's loyalty and interest in me had become a mere filament.

One day blended into the next. Working long hours alone in my home office day after day, I memorized the patterns of light throughout the day. The early morning sunlight illuminated the ceiling in an unbroken pattern. As the morning progressed, a shaft of light crawled down the wall, eventually breaking into smaller bands created by the mini-blinds in the window. Soon after reaching the floor, they disappeared, replaced by washed-out opaqueness. As the day progressed, the room took on increasingly darker hues. Finally, a golden shaft from the afternoon western sky pierced the house briefly, then bade goodbye as it sank behind a row of trees. With the sun gone, the house became a somber gray that slowly descended into darkness. The rooms were deathly quiet except for the occasional commotion of my furry little stalwart friends: Darby, Taka, and Sabrina. They were the "rocks" of my life. Cindy never called when she was gone or said much about where she'd been once she returned home.

In Cindy's defense, I wasn't easy to live with. In nearly constant pain, frustrated at my physical limitations, and stressed by the new job, I was irritable and short-tempered. Occasionally, we argued; more often than not, we didn't talk at all. She had her own interests and friends and turned increasingly to them. I found solace in classes and events at Unity Church.

Meanwhile, problems arose in my partnership with Dan, who had never worked with anyone. He couldn't understand why I had trouble understanding the complicated systems and techniques he had developed and used successfully in his self-owned firm. At times, his impatience showed how rocky our relationship had become. Everything was new to me and he wasn't a very good teacher. However, something even more insidious seemed to be at work: my brain continued to feel like porridge. Each mental task seemed to take longer than ever before. I was slow in comprehending things, especially new ideas.

I learned years later that the downstairs fall, as well as the seizure I experienced in the rehab hospital, may have caused brain damage. At any rate, there were twelve small "dead" areas called infarctions[1], essentially evidence of mini-strokes.

The second week of September was a special treat for me. For the first time since the accident, I returned to my hometown of Nelson, Nebraska, where I'd grown up. Seeing Mom and Dad again, renewing old friendships, and visiting the secret places I'd loved as a kid was a balm for my body and soul. For the first time since before the accident, I completely relaxed.

Coincidentally, on the fateful day of September 11, 2001, when terrorists attacked America, I succeeded in playing nine holes of golf. Afterward, as I was sitting on the back patio writing in a journal I'd kept for many years, Dad came out of the house to tell me something terrible had happened. Two planes had crashed into the World Trade Center in New York, killing many people. Terrorism was suspected. It was a senseless act of violence that represented pure hatred toward America and its ideals. Sadly, I wrote that until we, as a people, start listening and trying to understand one another, there will never be peace on this planet. Unfortunately, this shift in consciousness has never happened.

One day back in Olathe, a woman I knew was driving by and stopped to talk as I went to get the mail. She was a freelance journalist for the Olathe Daily News. When I told her my story, she said it sounded exciting and agreed to pass it along to her editor. A few days later, a reporter called and interviewed me and took a picture of Darby and me. The article ran on the front page of the paper and was entitled "Duo Gives Hope to Others," along with this picture:

Mike and Darby, October 2001

Before long, people with serious injuries began calling me asking for advice. I always fumbled for an answer. I wanted to tell them that

115

they had all the power from God they needed to maximize their healing, but I didn't know how to express this without sounding pompous or kooky.

A few weeks later, as I was sitting on the driveway filling cracks in the asphalt, a voice came from behind me. A lady driving by had recognized me from the picture in the paper and stopped, saying, "I just wanted to tell you I read the article about you in the Olathe paper, and it was so inspiring that I sent it to my sister, who has cancer. I know she'll appreciate it." I turned my head to thank her but never really saw the lady's face. I received several other calls from people who'd drawn strength from the article. It seemed as though the universe was helping me spread the message I had been given.

By October 2001, I no longer needed a cane even though I still had equilibrium problems and walked with a limp. Flush with optimism at my newfound freedom, I decided it was time to put my "bonus" objective of the year to the test: to walk ten miles. I'd been steadily increasing the distance of my walks since July, and it was up to three miles. But ten? I guess there's only one way to find out, I told myself: try it.

The next Saturday, I drove to the familiar trail where I'd done dress rehearsals for my Colorado mountain climbing adventures two years previously. Things started well until I realized too late that I'd forgotten to bring water. What a dumb mistake! Oh well, we don't need no stinking water! I joked. Gimping merrily, I noticed hikers of all ages continuously going around me because of my slow pace.

It was a crisp early fall morning, and the leaves on the trees hadn't begun to turn. Finally, the five-mile marker came into view. Halfway! My legs were holding up well, so I started the return trip after a short rest. However, the hills seemed bigger this time, and my pace slowed. After about seven miles, my left thigh began throbbing, feeling like an extra ten pounds had been added. Then, after eight miles, it happened: without warning, my knees buckled, sending me sprawling face-first onto the hard asphalt.

For several seconds, I lay stunned, pain spreading. Blood oozed from both knees and elbows. How am I going to get up? I groaned. Finally, I slowly pulled myself upright using one knee as a fulcrum. Embarrassed, cut, bloody, and with knees aching, I limped onward. At last, the car came into view. With a deep sigh, I staggered to it, opened the door, collapsed onto the seat, and with a bloodied pen crossed another goal off the list.

In November, I signed up to participate in a charity walk to raise money for Habitat for Humanity. Cindy declined an offer to join me. "Physical exercise isn't my thing," she said. Early one bright fall Saturday, several hundred of us gathered at the new riverfront park on the south banks of the Missouri River. Some had signed up to walk five miles, while others chose to run ten miles. I decided to go for ten miles but by walking not running. In the cool, invigorating morning breeze, I walked along the city streets admiring the architecture of older homes. Before long, the throng began to spread out. Naturally, I fell to the rear of the pack. But speed wasn't important. Rather, the goal was to finish the walk both for myself and those who had pledged money to me on behalf of Habitat for Humanity for every mile I walked.

My intensity was interrupted when, after about seven miles, the "little bell" went off in my head that I knew oh so well. Uh oh! It was time to find a restroom and the sooner, the better! Incontinence was one of the irritating side effects of my spinal injury. Fortunately, I found a restroom before the unthinkable happened.

Afterward, noticing there were few walkers in sight (meaning everyone else was far ahead), I decided it was time to turn back. My decision was a good one as I got a dirty look on the return route from a police officer who was holding traffic because of me. Eeek! I must be the last person in the event, I told myself, trying to pick up my pace. The result was minimal and only succeeded in making me appear more ridiculous as I hobbled along. Finally, a sidewalk came into view, and I quickly gravitated toward it to avoid bringing an entire section of the city to a halt.

Sometime later, the finish line (also the start line) mercifully came into view. A large crowd was listening to a speaker, so I could tell the day's events were just concluding. Reaching the crowd, I looked for an opening to dart into unnoticed. Too late. To my horror, the announcer laughingly yelled over the P.A., "Hey, let's give a big hand to our LAST walker of the day! Why not?" A smattering of applause arose from the large gathering, accompanied by a few laughs and indulgent smiles. Blushing, I whispered a few words of explanation into the ear of a guy standing near me and looked again for a way to disappear quickly into the crowd. The guy walked over to the speaker and whispered something to him. "Well," the speaker said, "I've just been told that our last walker suffered a spinal cord injury this year." This time, the applause was louder, and the smiles were different. Several people came to shake my hand.

In spite of the feel-good article in the Olathe paper, in spite of walking ten miles, and in spite of doing seven miles in the "Habitat for Humanity" walk, the extreme after-effects of the injury made life miserable. Every night was mostly a sleepless ordeal, bringing new meaning to the word "pain." I always welcomed the first morning light because it meant I'd made it through another excruciating night. Days weren't much better due to the meager earnings of my at-home job compounded by Cindy's increasingly frequent absences and tenuous explanations. When she finally came home, I was sulky and uncommunicative, which only caused the distance between us to expand.

In December, we received a letter from the University of Kansas that no parent ever wants to receive from their child's college. Despite his above-average intelligence and exceptional abilities, Sean wasn't doing well academically. I regretted we had allowed him to spurn offers from several smaller colleges to play football for them in favor of enrolling at KU and the temptations of a fraternity. Sean's college career ended prematurely and he returned home. It was a tremendous disappointment to us. While hopeful Sean would stand tall on firmer soil in the long run, it was a challenge that only he could overcome in his own time and in his own way.

Later that month, I drove to the Rehabilitation Institute to sign some stray insurance papers. As I was leaving the building, I noticed a sitting area in front of Trinity Hospital across the street. I strolled over to the little area. It was sparsely landscaped with a small bench, a few scraggly potted plants, and a much-used cigarette receptacle. While unremarkable to most people, standing there represented a monumental achievement for me. Only a few months earlier, sitting in my wheelchair, I'd gazed at the area longingly from my room on the second floor across the street. Back then, it seemed impossible that I'd ever stand on the spot where I'd gazed for so many hours. Stoically but with a lump in my throat, I returned to the car and slid into the driver's seat. When I turned on the ignition to leave, the following words came from a song on the radio:

I never did believe in miracles, But I've a feeling it's time to try.

I never did believe in the ways of magic, But I'm beginning to wonder why.[2]

How prophetic! I also had been blessed by miracles. It brought tears to my eyes. But the song also raised some questions. If a miracle happened once, what was I doing wrong to prevent more good things from happening?

Chapter 14
Strange Happenings

For years, I had survived difficult times by drawing upon a combination of stubbornness, determination, and a belief that somehow everything would turn out right in the end. But it wasn't easy—never, ever was it easy. And in spite of all that I'd learned about positive thinking, my mind was oftentimes filled with depressive, negative thoughts.

Whether it was the result of my mindset or something else, peculiar things began happening. It wasn't the first time I had experienced strange occurrences in my life, beginning as a kid in Nebraska. However, "things" had been quiet since the morning of my accident when I was awakened by a distinctively metallic female voice saying, "It's six o'clock." Groggily rousing myself, I went to the bedroom to look at the clock. You guessed it, it was exactly six a.m.

For the next several years following the accident, "they" were back—with greater intensity and frequency than ever before. Everyone in the house experienced strange phenomena, a few of which were:

- Loud bangs coming from everywhere in the house, day and night, sometimes several days in succession.
- Once, I made the mistake of asking whatever was in the house to do something to prove its presence. The next day, a Tiffany lamp weighing at least 10 pounds was lying on the floor beside its table. At first suspecting one of the animals had knocked it off, I realized it had been lifted over a large, undisturbed crystal ball on the table. I couldn't believe one of our cats could have knocked it off the table.
- In March of 2002, a severe ice storm hit Kansas City. Thousands of trees were damaged or destroyed, and the city shivered under a blackout for four days. Cindy was in warm San Francisco with her friend. The morning after the storm, I took some digital pictures of the exquisitely beautiful but

deadly ice-coated world. As I downloaded the photos onto the computer, I noticed something strange. About every fourth picture or so, there was one or more round, translucent object on the ground, in the sky, and even in trees. Varying in size and shape, ghostly contrails emanated from some and a few had features resembling human faces. The strangest was a globular sphere, about a person's height, in front of an apple tree in the backyard. The tree branches clearly showed through the luminescent object, and a wispy white column ran from the object to the ground, meaning it was either a part of the object or that the object was rapidly moving upward as the shutter clicked. These strange objects occasionally appeared in photographs for the next year or so, including some taken during appraisal assignments. Then, just as inexplicably as they began, the objects quit showing up, ruling out a camera defect. I later learned that "orbs" were being recorded worldwide, primarily on digital cameras. Theories of their cause range from dust particles to plasma energy to inter-dimensional partially manifested apparitions.[1]

- Over a six-month period, five goldfish vanished from our home aquarium without a trace—one, less than an hour after I'd purchased him and put him in the tank. The tank was covered so that the cat couldn't have eaten the fish, and it didn't seem plausible that one of my other old, lazy goldfish, many of which had been in the tank for five years, would suddenly turn carnivorous and eat one of their own. Nothing like this had happened in the 20 years we had an aquarium of goldfish.

- During a meeting where the host joked that the mansion where it was being held was haunted, I felt pain in my right hand. Looking down, I saw an indentation of the exact size and shape of a thumbnail on my right hand near the thumb. A few minutes later, my right arm began to bleed. When I got home, an ominous feeling permeated the house. More than one "something" was in the house. Several hours after going to bed, I sensed something come into the bedroom. The image of a man small in stature came to mind. I could even hear it breathing. The next day, Sabrina disappeared. For the next day and a half, I searched futilely for her by following a faint meow from nowhere but everywhere. Her food and water lay untouched. Finally, I found her cowering underneath my bed in fear. Fresh, slimy, putrid smelling feces was smeared all over the poor kitty's chest.

- Early one weekend morning, when Ryan was home alone, he was awakened by the sound of chanting coming from a tape in a portable tape player in the living room. The tape player had turned on by itself.

- Around 3:30 a.m. one night, Sean got up and went into the kitchen for a bowl of cereal. It was warm outside, and the window was open. While sitting at the table eating, he heard a weird noise like a child's kazoo coming from outside the window. Turning apprehensively to look, a face stared back at him from outside the window. As the window is roughly seven feet above the ground, it's doubtful it could have been a living being.

- As I was on my knees cleaning the glass shelf of a baker's rack, I removed two candle holders and placed them on the carpet behind me. After cleaning the glass, I reached for the candle holders to replace them on the shelf. One of the candle holders was gone.

Things got so disruptive that, at the risk of being labeled a kook, I contacted Barry, a psychic. Barry's credentials were impressive. Besides being a practicing attorney, he was an ordained rabbi and an experienced exorcist. Over the course of 25 years, he had conducted many ghost investigations and performed many exorcisms. I asked Barry if he would come to the house and do a reading.

A few nights later, there was a knock at my door. Opening it, there stood Barry in full exorcism regalia. Somewhat embarrassed, I let him inside, quickly glancing up and down the street, for fear that someone might have seen him, before shutting the door. While I knew something drastic needed to be done to put an end to the unwelcome happenings, my practical upbringing revolted at the idea of a bizarre ritual being performed in my house. Sean was watching TV downstairs at the time but never moved or said a word.

After writing a check for the $100 fee, Barry ceremonially set his Bible on the table, put his ceremonial exorcist scarf around his neck, and said a prayer in Latin. After doing a walk-through of the house, he concluded there were two entities in the house: one of a young man who had known me when I was young and wanted me to acknowledge his presence and the spirit of a Native American man who had been killed 300 years ago in a battle on our property. Through Barry, the young man said he pushed me down the stairs to get me to acknowledge him but never meant for me to be injured. Suddenly, the statement that "the poltergeist pushed me" immediately after the fall made sense.

Then, looking me straight in the eyes, Barry said darkly, "There also are 'other things' in this neighborhood that want you gone." He refused to be more specific but strongly advised me to place salt at the four corners of the property.

After performing a cleansing ritual in every room of the house, he ordered the entities to leave with the aid of Archangel Michael. He also sprinkled salt at the four corners of my property line and urged me to pray to Archangels Michael and Uriel to protect the property.

However, the one who pushed me down the stairs promised to stop being disruptive if I let him stay. Reluctantly, I agreed if "he" vowed to be "nice." But a few days later, bangs once again came from the basement. Even worse, yet another fish inexplicably disappeared from the aquarium. Shaken, I called Barry and told him what had happened. He agreed to come again but wanted another $100. "Well, in that case," I said, "don't bother. I'll find a way to handle it myself."

So what was the significance of all this paranormal activity? Was it because I had let my attitude become so open during the healing process that both positive and negative energies were manifesting? Or was it because the positive energy that had been so useful during my initial recovery period had been destroyed by the adverse events that took place afterward with my resulting negative attitude? Could it be that positive thinking creates positive results and negative thinking equally results in negative consequences? If so, what was the moral? As always, I searched for answers in the solitude of nature.

Sitting under a gigantic black oak tree at a favorite hideaway in a nearby nature park the following day, I pondered the question. There seemed to be a clear connection between my attitude and significant life events over the past few years. Fifteen months earlier, I had suffered a terrible physical injury that left the vast majority of patients with the same injury unable to walk. However, a positive attitude played a major role in defying the odds until I was almost "normal" again. But even with all that positive resolution at my disposal, more bad things happened in my life—weird paranormal stuff. Are positive and negative events the result of attitude, or are they random?

I recalled that in his book, "The Holographic Universe," Michael Talbot stated he also experienced many paranormal events in his life that coincided with his state of mind at the time. He says, "I have always accepted the idea that poltergeists are manifestations of the unconscious psychokinetic abilities of the person around whom they are most active."[2] As afternoon shadows lengthened, the answer became clear: don't let circumstances dictate your view of life. We have the power to control our perception of every event in our lives. So, why not think about happiness? Why not believe in abundance? This truth is demonstrated admirably in the movie The Secret,[3] which over and over demonstrates examples of the powerful effect of the Law of Attraction.[4]

Regardless of whether I had caused negative events to come into my life or it was just more of life's junk, I couldn't let myself become a victim. If I had somehow opened a "door," allowing dark forces to enter my life, I had the power to just as easily close that "door I didn't need a medium, an exorcist, a witch doctor, or anyone else to solve the problem. I had all I needed—inside. And when healing first began from my spinal injury, I knew the elimination of fear played a pivotal role.

Then and there, I banished all future paranormal activity from the house. However, since I wrote the first edition of this book in 2015, I have occasionally experienced paranormal activity. The activity seemed to increase as time went on, particularly just before a big event in my life. I don't know why this happens to me, and I have needed to remind myself of the lessons I previously learned. And after I do, my "visitors" don't stay for long.

Chapter 15
The "Miracle" of Healing

Throughout my recovery period, I continued learning more about the nature of the universe and how to unlock the hidden powers of the mind. Through the generosity of Brad and Diane Masters, I discovered a Japanese alternative healing method called Reiki[1]. The simple technique involved placing your hands on, or slightly above, a person's body to direct the Chi (life energy) in the body to areas that need healing.[2] I was amazed to find that, following a healing session, the left side of my body was significantly warmer than before and remained pain-free for several days, providing temporary but much-needed relief from the pain and turgidity that plagued me. A bonus was learning how to employ the technique myself, which worked just as well as a pain reliever. Brad and Diane also taught me new methods of mind control.

One day, Mom called to tell me about a young man living in a town not far from ours in Nebraska who had suffered a severe spinal injury as a result of a car accident. The doctors gave him little to no chance of ever walking again.

A few days later, I called Matt[3] in his hospital room in Lincoln, Nebraska. "Hello," he said slowly in a low-sounding voice. After introducing myself and asking about him, he said, "My spinal cord was stretched as a result of the accident, and the doctors told me I'll never walk again." Hearing this made me angry. "Don't listen to them," I said, "because they don't understand the effect the mind can have on healing!" I told him about my spinal injury and offered to send him some information on the topic. He sounded interested.

Over the next few months, Matt and I talked often on the phone. One day he excitedly told me about a program he'd heard about called "Project Walk" in Carlsbad, California. The program employed advanced therapy techniques, similar to those used by the actor Christopher Reeve. Amazing results were being achieved, even among patients with very serious spinal injuries. "What a difference compared to the doctors in Lincoln," he said. "All they wanted me to do was learn life skills so I could cope with living in a wheelchair."

The next time we talked, Matt had gone to the Project Walk treatment center in California. He told me the following remarkable story:

"When I got there, they put me on a table. The doctor said, 'OK, now swing your legs.'

"I can't," I told him.

"Why not?"

"Because they told me I couldn't."

"Well, do it anyway," he said nonchalantly.

"So I began trying to move my legs. For a long time, nothing happened, but all of a sudden, one of them twitched. I couldn't believe my eyes and thought it must have been a muscle spasm. But a few minutes later, it happened again. They continued to work with me for several days, and by the time I went home, I could move my legs more easily and frequently. Back in Nebraska, I went to Lincoln for a checkup. They wouldn't believe me when I showed them I could move my legs. 'It's got to be a muscle spasm,' one said. But when I continued to move them upon request, they became more and more amazed, finally calling other medical staff."

Matt returned to Project Walk several more times in the ensuing months and each time gained increased mobility. By August 2007, he was able to walk a block with his walker and soon thereafter made it up 25 steps with his walker folded up lengthwise on the steps and a handrail. Matt proved what science is discovering: *that the spinal cord is capable of learning in simple ways and that it changes in response to environmental cues.* Many investigators interpret this as a form of muscle memory. The point is, *these abilities remain even when the spinal cord is cut off from the brain.*[4]

Matt told me about a young man he had met from Clear Lake, Iowa, who also had a spinal injury. Matt tried to convince him to accompany him to California to visit the offices of Project Walk.

However, his mother said they couldn't afford it even though Matt's church offered to help some. "He wouldn't come," Matt said sadly. Unfortunately, this story has a tragic and ironic ending. Two years later, Matt was killed in a second automobile accident on the same road where he'd had the first accident. At the time of his death, he could walk a block with his walker and was preparing to attend college in Iowa that fall. What a tragedy!

I will never forget this amazing young man, whose courage and determination proved many of the so-called experts wrong. Although his death seemed terribly unfair, I'm sure it was part of a larger plan in his life that we mere mortals don't understand. All I know is that Matt is an example of what many who have had spinal cord injuries can achieve. His message to never give up hope or take no for an answer is one that should not be forgotten. He proved that through faith, belief and a refusal to give up, anything is possible!

Maybe someday everyone will know this—even young men from Clear Lake, Iowa, with spinal cord injuries who were told they would never walk again.

On several occasions, I visited patients at two major medical institutions to speak with those who had suffered spinal injuries. My message was always the same: *through faith, belief in the possible, hard work, and refusing to give up, there are unlimited possibilities.* The only restrictions are those we place upon ourselves. While the patients seemed to appreciate the message, it soon became evident that some people at the institutions didn't approve of what I was telling their patients. The validity of my recovery was openly challenged, and soon after, the invitations stopped coming. One supervisor, when asked, explained that they feared I might give their patients excessive hope.

Can a person have too much hope? And, more pointedly, what is "hope"? Could it be that there are as many definitions of hope as there are people in the world? We all have different ambitions, desires, motivations, and goals, and only we know the secret to our sense of joy. For some, it may be conquering a physical challenge; for others, it's overcoming mental challenges. However, for yet others, happiness is spiritual in nature. But whether you find joy in climbing a mountain, running a marathon, sculpting a statue, writing or singing a beautiful song, or simply being one with nature while appreciating all the grace and beauty the universe has to offer, it's all equally good. *A "miracle" is anything that brings lasting joy and peace of mind to the individual.* There are no right or wrong answers, only those that are in the best interests of your soul. As it says in the first paragraph of Reinhold Niebuhr's "Serenity Prayer," which is read before every 12-Step program: "God, grant me the serenity to accept the things I cannot change; courage to change the things I can; and wisdom to know the difference."[5]

In his book, "The Physics of Miracles,"[6] Richard Bartlett states, "If you don't like what your life experience is showing you, drop down into the sacred space of your heart and from this vantage point ask, 'If I were to begin to have a new experience in life, what would it look like and feel like?'"

I had come to understand that everything in the universe, including us, is made entirely of vibrational energy. This vibrational energy is fed by our emotions, which communicate the message, good or bad, to our physical body. Science has shown that the number of neuron receptors in our cells increases in response to a particular emotion. *I felt that one of the keys to healing was to release the negative emotional perceptions that bind the body in shackles and replace them with wholeness and wellness.* Or, in Christian terms, "Let go and let God." By trusting that the universe hears your entreaty, you will see how life can change for you. Through my growing understanding of the relationship between science and spirituality, I realized that miracles are everywhere if we just open our eyes to see them! *Creating miracles is simply a matter of disregarding previous ideas of limitation, releasing emotions, creating goals, and installing the intention into your consciousness as though it already has happened. By doing so, your consciousness transcends to a higher level.*

The book "Remarkable Recovery" is filled with stories of patients with serious or terminal diseases who used a variety of techniques to heal themselves. These techniques ranged from laughter therapy to visualizing cancer cells as alien spacecraft in a video game that you shot with your space ray gun. The specifics don't matter. What DOES matter is that the patients created a vision of whole and perfect health. But more than belief, they felt in their hearts that healing had come to pass. They then released their intention and let the universe handle the details.[7]

A number of scientifically controlled experiments have demonstrated the effect the mind has on healing, not only upon ourselves but on virtually any other living thing as well. Experiments by Dr. Daniel Benor showed that thoughts can have powerful effects on a variety of plants, seeds, single-celled organisms such as bacteria and yeast, insects, and other small animals.[8]

Leonard Laskow, an American gynecologist and healer, asked American biologist Glen Rein to perform a series of tests to determine the most effective healing strategy for inhibiting cancer cell growth. Rein prepared five different Petri dishes containing an identical number of cancer cells. In the first two tests, Laskow was asked to send a different intention to each Petri dish while holding it in his hands. In the final test, he held each intention while grasping one of five vials of water that would later be used to make up the tissue-culture medium of the cancer cells.

The five intentions used were as follows:

a) that the natural order be reinstated and the cells' growth rate return to normal,
b) Taoist visualization that only three cancer cells remained living in the Petri dish,
c) simply ask God to have His will flow through Laskow's hands,
d) maintain a state of love and compassion, and
e) visualize the cells dematerializing, going into either the light or the "void."

Rein measured the amount of radioactive thymidine absorbed by the cancer cells to measure the effectiveness of each approach, which is an indicator of the growth rate of malignant cells. Laskow's various intentions had significantly different effects. While both positive and negative connotations worked, the most powerful were those framed in a request combined with a highly specific visualization of the outcome that was not necessarily destructive. As Lynne McTaggart wrote in *The Intention Experiment*, "With healing, the most effective approach may not be to destroy the source of the illness but to move aside, let go of the outcome, and allow a greater intelligence to restore order."[9]

Ours is a "living" universe comprised of intelligent energy. Whether viewed from an atheistic/agnostic, secular, religious/spiritual, or scientific perspective, creation is filled with grace and offers unlimited possibilities for each of us. But regardless of our perspective, the key to unlocking the limitations of body and soul we've been taught since we were children is to open our hearts and trust that we deserve what we desire.[10]

As the Bible says in Mathew 7:7-8:

"Ask, and it will be given to you; search and you will find; knock and the door will be opened for you. For everyone who asks receives, and everyone who searches finds, and for everyone who knocks, the door will be opened."

Regardless of our desires or definition of happiness, know that all can be achieved. None of us can ever have "too much" hope or have to settle for anything less than what we truly want in life.[11]

Many of the world's religions consider their beliefs the only path to God; miracles such as healing can be achieved through them. Others, such as Gnosticism[12] and New Thought,[13] believe we're co-creators with God and that anything is possible through faith, belief, and action. Finally, proponents of natural law such as *the Law of Attraction,*[14] as expressed in the movie *The Secret,*[15] believe a frequency corresponding to our way of thinking is sent out into the universe and attracts back to us events and circumstances on that same frequency.

Notice the similarity? Faith is required for our prayers to be answered, and if there's any doubt that complete wholeness is acceptable, healing will not be realized. There are no limits to the power of faith.

The difference is that people of some faiths believe the key to miracles is to turn everything over to their deity or to hold positive thoughts. I am reminded of a song sung by Janis Joplin, "Oh Lord, won't you bring me a color TV..." For these people, when their desires aren't realized or if bad things continue to happen in their lives, they either blame it on God as retribution for not having sufficient faith or upon Satan, a universal force that is opposed to God and whose purpose is to destroy them physically, emotionally and spiritually. For these people, the world can look like a terrifying place with a constant struggle between light and dark, good and evil. As Gregg Braden writes in his book, "The Spontaneous Healing of Belief," "To internalize the belief that two forces with different agendas are battling is to invite the combat into our bodies and our lives." This belief that an evil force is working against us can inhibit healing because it creates doubt in our minds. The key is to realize that there aren't two forces in the world but rather one single force that works in many ways to create the experiences of our lives. Once we do this, the force will become unified, and our judgments toward ourselves and others will disappear.[16]

As these limitations fall away, a new world of possibilities emerges. It is a world in which, by combining faith with a commitment to action, God will manifest through us, creating infinite possibilities.

The Disciple Peter, at his Master's bidding, did the seemingly impossible by walking on water until he began doubting his Divinity, became frightened, and began to sink. Immediately reaching out his hand and catching him, Jesus said, "You of little faith, why did you doubt?" (Mat 14:28)

From a scientific standpoint, the secrets of the universe are being revealed, layer upon layer, at an increasingly rapid pace. According to Google CEO Eric Schmidt, every two days, we create as much information as we did from the dawn of civilization up until 2003.[17] Likewise, the basis of healing is coming closer to being understood. Once fanciful theories such as Jung's *collective unconsciousness*[18] and an omniscient energy field variously referred to as Torsion, Od, or Subtle Energy, and the Zero Point Field,[19] will be proven. Other theories, such as David Bohm's "Implicate" and "Explicate" orders,[20] and string theory,[21,22] may provide keys to answering many questions regarding the nature of God and the universe.

Perhaps one of the most profound connections between science and spirituality is the nature of light itself. Consider this: light represents the cornerstone of special relativity and all modern physics, and it exists outside of space and time. Light is a major feature of near-death experiences; it exhibits an uncanny and unexplained awareness (consciousness) of its surroundings and occurs instantaneously (faster than light).[23,24] Correspondingly, many religious texts equate God to light. As Jesus said, "I am the light of the world; he who follows me will not walk in darkness but will have the light of life" (John 8:12). And John 1:5 says, "This is the message we have heard from him and proclaim to you, that God is light and in him is no darkness at all."

Another connection between science and spirituality is beautifully expressed in *The Universe Story* by Thomas Berry and Brian Swimme:

If the expansion (of the universe) had been a little bit slower, the universe would have collapsed into an enormous black hole. Or if the expansion had just been a little bit faster, the universe would have expanded just too fast for the galaxies to form, and we'd simply have dust. If you altered the expansion by just one millionth of one percent, the entire universe would collapse. So, it suggests a profound wisdom at work in the universe.[25]

Regardless of the name people use for it, I believe there is a divine presence at work in the universe. I believe the day will come when humankind will know "how God thinks,"[26] as Einstein sought all his life. This unification will not diminish religious terminology such as, *The Kingdom, the Power, and the Glory of God.*[27] Rather, it will support scientific evidence that there is no time or space, that everything is connected and part of an omniscient force called God. In addition, consciousness plays a vital role in creating our universe.

Through this understanding, previously unexplained "miracles" such as healing will be understood. It will mark an evolution in

133

consciousness that results in a healthier, happier existence for humankind.

Chapter 16
Not If, When

It had not been a good day. I was working on the latest appraisal assignment at my partner's home office; the atmosphere was more tense than usual, reflecting the differences in our personalities that had become increasingly pronounced over time. Late in the day, as I was preparing to leave, he made yet another thinly veiled, sarcastic, derogatory comment toward me. Without responding, I knew this was the last straw and that our association was over.

Briefcase in hand, I limped slowly to my car for the drive home. Angrily opening the door, I tossed the briefcase and watched with satisfaction as it hit the far door and bounced, sending its contents flying. Wearily slumping into the driver's seat, I placed my hands on the wheel and buried my head between them. After a few moments of silence, realizing yet another disappointment, I turned the ignition key. The car awoke from its slumber and slowly moved away from Dan's house for the last time.

As the car crept along the residential streets, a montage of thoughts and images filled my mind. For months, I'd employed every job search technique I knew to find a better position, to no avail. It was as though the universe had placed a boulder in my path, blocking every turn. I'm never going to find my place in the world again. It's hopeless. While many chains had fallen, others remained.

Yes, I could walk, but many effects of the spinal injury remained. At least other members of the household had become used to my screams of pain in the dead of the night. My physical recovery had stalled. My left side still felt five pounds heavier than the right, and each time I stood up, my body quivered uncontrollably for several moments. Every step I took required a conscious effort to lift my left leg to keep from tripping, sometimes unsuccessfully. Other times, a knee would give out without warning, sending me flat on my face. I had tried to run many times, but the results were pitiful, if not pathetic—unless contorting one's body back and forth like a land crab for 50 yards is considered "running." My motivation literally came one step at a time. The lesson was both a curse and a blessing. Perhaps the conventional medical world was right, and I'd gone as far as possible. After all, more than a year had passed since the time of my spinal injury.

In spite of all the inspirational stories of success by other people with serious injuries, I had hit a plateau. Complete recovery seemed increasingly beyond my reach. I had come so close, recovering roughly 90% of my functions. You would have thought that I would fully recover in light of all I'd learned. But it didn't happen that way. One day, I can't remember the exact date, I said, "Well, you've done better than they ever thought possible. Things aren't all that bad. At least they're tolerable. Might this be good enough?" That day marked the end of my physical improvement from the spinal injury. It proved that the key to success is 100% unqualified certainty! Even the shadow of doubt can stop or delay the process.

Driving along the freeway that Friday afternoon of May 22, 2002, I toyed with this idea: I'm tired of pushing myself. Why not just let go? I'm tired of putting myself through this. I longed deeply for the peace of mind of "just being."

However, rather than finding solace in the idea, the closer I got to home the angrier I became. What had I done to deserve the past fourteen months of hell I'd suffered: a broken neck, paralysis, job layoff, permanent physical impairments, constant pain, and a deteriorating marriage? Despite all the revelations and insights I had regarding God and the nature of the universe, my mind reverted to an earlier time and railed: "I know I'm not a perfect person, but why am I being punished? What do you want from me, God? I don't deserve this. To hell with what anybody else thinks or believes about me, I'm not giving up!"

Then it occurred to me that sometimes the best way to get what you want warrants letting go. This doesn't mean quitting, not having a plan, or being less determined. Sometimes, less is more. While I knew there would be physical limitations, nothing could stop me from accomplishing what I wanted in life if I set my mind to it.

The Bible states, and many theologians agree, that the universe is abundant and wants each of us to succeed. But to receive, one must ask. Was now the time to ask? At first, my old skepticism and perhaps a bit of leftover foolish pride resurfaced. In spite of my healing and previous experience with a Novena, I still put great stock in the ability of my own willpower to overcome physical issues. Maybe I was a slow learner.

Then, I recalled something from Reiki called a "God box." The idea was simple: choose a box or container that's sacred or special to you, write down your wishes, desires, or intentions, place them in the box, and then "let go and let God." It's worth a try, I sighed. I surely could use some help now.

That night, in the back of a bureau, I found a beautiful three-by-four-inch carved box that I had but had not used for years. After dusting off the forgotten artifact and placing it on a table, I wrote the following on a piece of paper:

(1) Obtain a good job with a good salary, and

(2) Run a mile.

Ceremoniously, I folded the paper, placed it inside the box, and closed the lid. Reverently but firmly, I put my hands on either side of the box, shut my eyes, and visualized both goals. However, I didn't pray "to" God. Instead, I "claimed" what I felt in my heart was mine all along: a self-satisfying and abundant life as well as the joy of running. With passion in every fiber of my being, I RESOLVED it wasn't IF these things were going to occur; it was WHEN. I then released the intention to God.

Over the next week, I took the God box down from the shelf several times a day, placed my hands on it, closed my eyes, and envisioned the intentions as though they'd already been achieved. Freely and effortlessly, I ran down country roads with my hair blowing in the wind. I believed in my financially rewarding job because it was spiritually fulfilling.

The following Tuesday, I called the personnel office of the federal agency regarding the job I'd applied for as an appraiser. The job had everything I wanted; I felt sure I would at least get an interview. Nervously, I inquired about the status of the position. "I'm sorry," came the impersonal-sounding voice on the other end, "we've already made a recommendation for that position."

Crushed! Why didn't I at least warrant an interview? Had they found out about my physical problems, and had someone said something against me? Was God still seriously pissed off at me? The beacon of hope I'd held onto for weeks flickered and dimmed, but I couldn't let myself wallow in self-pity. The news had to be viewed as yet another curve in the road to overcome.

Pulling myself together, I went to Joplin, Missouri, a few days later to complete one final appraisal for Dave. That night after dinner, I sat staring absently out the window of my motel room onto the road leading to the parking lot. I wonder how far that road goes? I pondered. Partly out of boredom and partly out of curiosity, I decided to see how far I could run down it. After changing clothes, I left the motel and walked to the road. It was a nice but cool evening, the kind I most used to enjoy when jogging prior to my injury. But this run wasn't to be as pleasurable.

Resolutely, I set out down the road doing my best to look like a normal person out jogging. The results weren't exactly as I'd hoped. My body lurched from side to side at a pace barely faster than most people walk. To make things worse, a killdeer bird landed a short way away and began outpacing me. "Quit mocking me, you stupid bird," I exclaimed out loud. With each step, I strained to lift my left leg above the pavement to swing it in front, hoping I wouldn't trip, fall, and make a fool of myself.

Up a gentle incline of the road, I lumbered with all the gracefulness of a baby hippo. Surprisingly, I wasn't completely spent after about a hundred yards, so I kept going. Wow, this is the farthest yet! After about five minutes, I came to a stop sign, gingerly turned around, and headed back toward the motel. The motel finally came into view. I jogged all the way to the door of my room. Eagerly getting into my car, I retraced my route. A half mile! I stared down at the odometer in disbelief. Wow, this is more than they told me I could ever do!

In the days to follow, I continued the ritual of placing my hands on the God box to feel the result of my two desires. However, I didn't try to force the outcome through willpower. Yes, I wanted a good job and the ability to run again, but rather than just "wanting" these things to happen, my heart felt as though both had already come to pass. I was simply waiting for the details. In spite of the good feelings, I knew it was important to be proactive in making my dreams become reality. If an ad for a promising job appeared, I quickly applied, and each night, I "ran" a little farther than the night before.

Nothing much happened the first week. Three days into the second week, however, the phone rang while I was working at home. I recognized the voice on the other end. It was the personnel director at the government agency with whom I'd spoken ten days earlier. After reintroducing herself, she said, "Mike, I'm calling to offer you the job of Review Appraiser with our office in Kansas City, Kansas." The salary she offered was more than twice the amount I'd earned the previous year working on my own.

For several long seconds, I could not speak. Then, in what may have been one of the most ignoble responses to a job offer ever, I began repeating over and over, "Are you kidding me? Are you kidding me?" I hadn't even had an interview, but when I pointed out this obvious fact to her, she said my qualifications were clearly superior to the other applicants and that an interview would only have delayed getting Washington's approval to offer me the job, thereby increasing the risk of losing me in the interim. Inwardly, I chuckled. If only she knew. But I wasn't about to question the rationale and quickly answered, "Yes, I'll take the job." After hanging up the phone, I let out a yell of joy, picked up Darby, Sabrina, and Taka in turn, and, to their mortification, danced around the room with them in my arms.

How swiftly life can change! Moments earlier, I'd been earning subsistence wages with no health insurance or retirement program, with little indication that the situation would change. Suddenly, all those problems were gone. Poof! Perhaps the greatest irony was that one of the duties of my new job would be to provide housing to disadvantaged people, including those with disabilities similar to my own. God does indeed work in mysterious ways.

The first of my two intentions had been met. When Cindy came home that evening, I excitedly told her the big news. She was happy but seemed strangely subdued. Perplexed, I studied her silently but didn't ask why her reaction was so muted. I started to say, "Come on, get your coat, let's go out to dinner," as we'd always done to celebrate significant events in our lives, but I hesitated. While we desperately needed a break from the months of financial stress that had placed further strain on our relationship, my practical side rebelled. It would be at least two weeks before I received a paycheck, and we simply didn't have the money. It made sense to hold off until that time. So without a word, I resolved we would wait and celebrate with my first paycheck. In retrospect, it may have been one of the biggest mistakes of my life.

The following morning the phone rang. It was from a bank recruiter calling in response to a vacancy I had applied for several weeks earlier. The recruiter sounded extremely interested in my resume and wanted me to come in for an interview. But even though I felt sure the salary would be more than the one I'd been offered with the government agency, I told him I had accepted another position. I had been burned before by the callousness and indifference of a private-sector corporation breaking promises that drastically affected our family's lives, and I had no desire for that to ever happen again. The disappointment in the man's voice was unmistakable.

Something had changed. Suddenly, it seemed as though the universe had opened itself to a new world of possibilities. However, even in this moment of great excitement, I didn't lose sight of the fact that it had taken me many years of hard work to set the stage for this "miracle" to happen.

Two days later, it was time to try jogging again. This was the BIG one—a mile! I chose an isolated road with little traffic. After parking the car, I squinted to see the one-half-mile point, which seemed more like ten miles in the distance. Oh well, I'll just take it one step at a time. After a silent prayer, away I went. The lead weight seemed to be strapped to my left leg again. With each step I concentrated on lifting my left leg to clear the pavement. Still, a loud scraping sound now and then let me know I wasn't managing very well.

At first, things didn't seem so bad. I enjoyed looking at the pretty fields on either side of the road. But after a while, the familiar heaviness and pain in my left side increased. While I was intently studying the ground in front of my feet, the shadow of a stop sign eventually came into sight, marking the halfway point of my journey. So far, so good. *This is the farthest I've gone so far. Now, can I make it back to the car?*

Before long, the muscles in my leg and hip began to burn. The pain spread throughout my body. With each additional step, the heaviness on my left side grew heavier. No longer able to enjoy the sight of the fields, I furrowed my brow and studied the tiny rocks embedded in the asphalt. At first, the closer I studied them, the more their uniqueness and beauty jumped out at me. *How can such wondrous things be?* I mused. *There has to be an intelligence behind it all, doesn't there?* The closer I studied each rock glistening up at me before passing underfoot, the more I became enamored by the tiny entities with lifelike qualities. Suddenly, I remembered the revelation I'd gotten on a hot summer night long ago and far away-- everything is "one." Me, you, the rocks, the galaxies, the tacos—it's all right here, right now: a gigantic hologram. And, as in a hologram, the entirety of the whole is contained in each and every part. Quantum mechanics has shown there is no separation between physical objects or between time's past, present, and future. Everything is merely a different aspect of "one." Plodding along the pavement, I smiled at the remembrance of this truth. I admired each aspect of the microcosmic universe with new eyes as it disappeared slowly underneath my feet.

Although my pace was embarrassingly slow, it didn't matter. Nothing mattered except the fact that I was close to realizing a goal I had visualized for many months, so giving up wasn't an option. Chains of the mind were falling! After what seemed a surprisingly short period of time, the tiny image of my car came into view. With renewed vigor, I tried to pick up the pace, but doing so increased the stress on various muscles and exaggerated my already abnormal gait.

With mostly shut eyes and gritted teeth, I ignored the fire raging inside my muscles. I had to keep going until I either fell on my face or reached the finish line. Each time I snuck a peek at the tiny car, it seemed only slightly larger than before, as was the stop sign behind it--my finish line. With each step, the heaviness in my left leg increased while the grating of my left foot against the pavement grew louder. The constant grating began ringing in my head.

Something funny then happened. All pain disappeared. It was as though I had separated from my body. More minutes passed, and now I could read the welcome word on the sign: "Stop." I couldn't stop looking at that one word until finally, it was beside me. I'd done it! Totally spent, I wobbled crazily toward the car and collapsed beside it before finally regaining enough strength to open the door and get into the driver's seat.

Hours and several pain pills later, my energy returned along with the implications beginning to sink in. I recalled telling my physical therapist at the Rehab Institute of my plans to jog and climb mountains again, followed by his slightly amused response: "That's great, Mike, but why don't we try to get you walking first." And later: "Honestly, you might be able to get around without a walker someday, but running or climbing mountains is going to be next to impossible." I recalled my soft response, "I'll send you a picture."

Until now, I hadn't realized the seeds of doubt the words had sown in my mind even though they weren't meant to be harmful. And even though additional challenges were yet to be conquered, the strength of the words was gone. While it had to be one of the ugliest one-mile runs in history, I felt like a football runner who had outmaneuvered his last defender while the only thing between the goal line was green grass! If they were wrong about my being able to run again, what else are they wrong about? Why not run two, three, or even four miles? In fact, what's to stop me from doing anything I set my mind to doing? Silently, I crossed off the second vow.

It later occurred to me that both of my intentions—to run a mile and get a permanent, professional job—had been achieved within two weeks of setting them. After many months of futile effort, why, I asked myself, do some wishes come true and others don't? It's one of the profoundest mysteries in life and one that's been debated for eons. Despite all my healing accomplishments, other aspects of my life had remained stuck for many months.

My circumstances only changed when I absolutely, positively resolved, without the slightest bit of doubt, that they could not continue on their present course. Wanting something to happen wasn't good enough. **What was required, it seemed, was a subtle but powerful shift from "wishing" to "feeling" as though the event had already occurred. However, as in the Novena prayer, I foresaw myself as complete and whole rather than achieving a specific outcome. This was in spite of the fact that the physical portion of my recovery had ceased.**

For millennia, enlightened spiritual beings have told us that the secret to miracles lies in combining thought and emotion while knowing that spiritual sources support you. We must see "something other" with our senses and live in the joyous end result. But equally important is to feel uncompromisingly what it's like when the project is completed. When we focus on what our lives would be like if our dreams were already fulfilled, we are actually creating the conditions within us that allow our fulfilled dreams to surround us.[1] In addition, numerous scientifically controlled experiments have shown that emotion must be linked to a loving intelligence and in the best interests of all. This "formula" works regardless of whether the desired result is directed toward you, another person, other living objects, or even natural events.[2]

But rather than trying to "force" something to happen, the key is to let go and let it happen. We've become accustomed to an external world created by consciousness through projection. But in the process, we forget who we really are: spiritual beings with the power to create reality as we desire. By aligning our consciousness with that of the living energy universe, we can take back the power we've always possessed. Science shows that this resonance is a fundamental law of the universe, one that is key to opening a world of possibilities. But there's a difference between "knowing" and "believing." "Knowing" something is stable and unchanging while believing can be changed through perception. If based on love and for the highest good, changing perception allows our desires to manifest. Through this technique, nothing is impossible except the limitations we place upon ourselves.

Chapter 17
End of an Era

The first morning of my new job, I awoke with a hop in my step and a song in my heart that had been silent for a long time. Having to get up early, put on dress clothes and actually "go" somewhere felt strange but good. Now, one paycheck would equal about four of what I had been getting the past nine months. Most importantly, the timing couldn't have been better, as financial disaster was staring us in the face.

A few days before starting the job, I received an invitation to travel to Pennsylvania where an international gathering of Clan McCord was celebrating the Fourth of July. It was an opportunity to meet people I'd known for many years but had never met in person and to accept a "Distinguished Service Award" for my book, The McCord Saga. I had even been asked to perform several honorary functions on behalf of the Clan. It was a once-in-a-lifetime opportunity, culminating 25 years of family history research that I simply couldn't afford to pass up.

Given our limited financial situation, it wasn't practical for Cindy to come as she wasn't interested in family history. I decided that when I got home, I would take her to dinner at a fancy restaurant, order a great bottle of wine, and thank her for hanging tough with me through the roughest period in our 29-year marriage. I felt she would be pleased.

On Tuesday, July 2, I flew out of Kansas City International for Harrisburg, Pennsylvania, and then to Lancaster County. The gathering was everything I had expected, with McCord representatives from all around the world. The countryside was beautiful. The places we visited, such as a small Presbyterian Church where my family worshipped in 1725, as well as McCord's Fort (which was attacked by Indians in 1756), were every bit as magical as I had always imagined. I even managed to sneak in a trip to the Gettysburg Battlefield on the Fourth of July, arriving shortly after the completion of commemoration activities of the battle that took place July 3-5, 1863.

As I enjoyed these activities, I began to unwind a bit, which made me realize how much stress I'd been under the past 15 months. What a ride it had been! Finally, good times were ahead! As a peace offering, I bought Cindy a beautiful handmade Amish woolen comforter as a gesture of my commitment to repairing our relationship. I planned to give it to her when I walked in the door.

I arrived back in Kansas City late in the day on Friday, July 5, feeling as relaxed and confident about the future as before my accident 17 months earlier. But I could sense something was different. When I turned the key in the lock and opened the door, the house was strangely quiet. After closing the door behind me, I saw a note from Cindy. It read:

Mike:

I've moved out. In the past year, I have become a different person. Love the boys, and I hurt them, too. You can do great things.

Cindy

For several long minutes, I stared at the white piece of paper without moving, then slumped into a chair in the living room and stared vacantly out the picture window. A myriad of thoughts and emotions flashed through my mind that Darby's joyful greeting couldn't overcome. While shocking, in truth, it wasn't terribly surprising. What was surprising was that she left a 29-year relationship by way of a short note without a single word of forewarning or any attempt to resolve things. While the past fifteen months had been by far the most difficult time in our 29-year marriage, I wasn't ready to give up on us, particularly now that I had a good job again. Life was finally about to become so much easier. The house felt cold and quiet as death. My mind was numb. Losing track of time, the shadows around me grew longer.

Not knowing what to do with the handmade Amish wool comforter, I took it to the store in the mall where her friend Judy worked. I regretted not seeing Cindy's face when she got the comforter because I knew she would be pleased.

For days, I tried to contact Cindy at the number where Ryan said she could be reached in the hope we could talk things out, but the woman answering the phone always said icily, "Cindy's not here." I truly felt that things could still be worked out if we could just sit down and talk. Later, I learned it was Cindy's friend, Judy, who kept me from talking to her, thus solidifying the third major calamity in my life in the past 15 months. I was, and remain, convinced that her special friend Judy was partially responsible for our breakup.

I was served divorce papers a month later, which brought a new kind of nightmare. Ours wasn't going to be a friendly divorce. With my new job as an excuse, and upon her friend's advice, Cindy pursued every available legal angle to get as much money from me as possible. This was the start of a legal and financial ordeal that knew no limits or bounds.

To further complicate this newest mess, I hired an attorney who turned out to be corrupt and incompetent. In a matter of three weeks, he bilked me out of $1,000, gave legal advice that resulted in my being charged with "contempt of court" for not paying temporary alimony on time, then disappeared. I fired him. He was later disbarred, and it would be more than a year before I got my money back—long after his damage had been done. Although I was not fined or put in jail because of the "contempt of court" ruling, my recently found faith in humanity was shattered. Forget all the positive thinking "crap," this is the last straw!

The following months might have been comical had the consequences not been so dire. At my new attorney's guidance, I spent many hours preparing evidence that was never even introduced in court to help my case. Motions followed countermotions; court extension followed court extension. Too late, I learned both attorneys were playing a well-rehearsed game, one that generated thousands of dollars in legal costs for both sides of the case. The last "laugh" came when I finally realized that the antiquated divorce laws of Kansas are astonishingly simple. Aside from being blatantly biased against the primary breadwinner, our divorce could have been resolved in minutes at a tiny fraction of the money we paid. We were victims of a legal game designed to make lawyers rich—one that cost more than $30,000 in attorney fees—money that had taken painstaking years to save for our sons' college educations.

Finalized on February 7, 2003, the divorce ironically occurred two years to the day of my injury. I would have been left homeless had it not been for a series of extraordinary events.

Two months before the final divorce decree, the house—like our marriage—began falling apart. Huge cracks appeared in the foundation. Walls separated, and scary cracks erupted along the basement, garage, and driveway floors. Not my house, too, I thought as I dialed an FHA inspector. He came early one Saturday morning and looked the place over carefully, inside and out, taking notes all the while. After he finished, he looked me in the eye while shaking his head slowly. "This is bad. You've got significant movement throughout the foundation. It's going to cost you more than $60,000 to fix these problems." After he left, I couldn't help chuckling with gallows humor: Let's hear it for my crumbling world!

As instructed by the court, I ordered a property appraisal. The new value came in at 46% less than the former appraisal. The court accepted the new appraisal and it became part of the settlement. In addition to getting half the value of all assets, the court gave Cindy a huge amount for alimony based on my new salary, from which I had not received a single check. It would take ten years to pay. I was financially ruined.

In order to sell the house, I had to complete at least some of the repairs. So I called a contractor to get an estimate. After looking things over, he hit upon a different way of doing the repairs that would cost around $12,000 rather than the $60,000 estimated by the FHA inspector. After a week of installing piers, jackhammering, and pouring new concrete, my contractor finished the work. Still thinking I'd need to sell, I ordered a new appraisal. To my astonishment, the value came in $5,000 more than the original amount. In short, there had been a cumulative 90% swing in value within a span of four months at precisely the time that I needed it the most. How is such a thing possible? It seemed as though it was divine intervention.

As a result, rather than having to sell the house, I refinanced the mortgage at a payment I could afford while realizing enough money to pay the enormous alimony settlement Cindy had been given. Because of this, the boys and I were able to continue living in our home of 15 years.

What were the odds of all these things happening the way they did in such short order and at precisely the right time needed to save me from financial ruin and preserve a home for my sons and me? Astronomical! I am absolutely convinced it was divine intervention.

While my experience with the legal system was unnecessarily contentious and nearly ruined me financially, Cindy and I were now free to build new lives separate from one another.

Chapter 18
Healing the Soul

They say time heals. I hoped so with all my heart. The past two years had been a roller coaster of lows, highs, and lows again. In spite of all I had learned, I was exhausted. My life had been torn apart, piece by piece. My soul ached. If life was a prize fight, I felt staggered up against the ropes and pummeled. However, I had taken every blow and refused to go down.

Recovering the parts of my soul that life had torn away would take years but as the dust settled, I began to see that even losing my partner of nearly 30 years was for the best. It was as though "God" had pushed the reset button in my life to remind me who I was and my purpose for being. It had taken tough love for me to remember some important truths I had lost sight of on the road of life: we are divine beings, love is the most important force in the universe, and we should be thankful for every moment because everything can be taken from us in the wink of an eye. The wind blowing in the high branches of the many majestic trees in our yard was a balm on my wounded soul and seemed to whisper to me, "Welcome home. We're glad you are still with us."

Another year began as a world of snow and ice, but when February 2003 turned to March, one of our fondest harbingers of spring, frogs in a nearby draw, began their timeless croaking as they awoke from their long winter's nap. The sound was my lullaby. Before long, trees swelled with new buds. Then came the familiar serenade of another old friend, the robin, whose melody was sweet music to the ear. But it wasn't until the crack of thunder from the first storm that spring officially announced its arrival. Could the earth's rebirth be a harbinger of things to come?

Ryan was nearing the end of his junior year in college. He continued living at home when not in school. He joined Sean, who had also moved back home after leaving college. It was comforting having the boys with me. To provide them a safe harbor from a harsh and cruel world was deeply gratifying. Most of the savings for their educations were gone (much of it to the attorneys); however, I vowed to use what little was left, along with whatever else it would take, to make sure Ryan could finish college and give Sean a second chance, should he decide to take it.

For the first time in over two years, the siege began to loosen. Nearly every aspect of my world looked different. I had recovered around 90% of my motor functions, had a better job than before the injury, and survived a bitter divorce. Now I was free to pursue new adventures and long-dormant passions.

I wanted to do more to help others facing life challenges, protect the environment, travel, and continue to grow spiritually. But more than anything else, I wanted to live every moment of the second chance in life I had been given.

This was a time of healing. The new job was going well, and new ideas brimmed forth daily. Meanwhile, I did my best to renew the love bonds between Sean and Ryan that had been strained as a result of years of division within the family along with the lengthy, acrimonious divorce process. My sons were innocent victims who had for years been caught in the middle of something that wasn't their fault or doing. The scars were deep. I knew it would take years, if ever, for them to fully heal.

There was one more thing to accomplish before I could put the awful events of the past few years behind me, something I had vowed to do prior to the injury: climb Mt. Elbert. An internet search revealed more about the challenge:

Name: In honor of Colorado statesman Samuel Hitt Elbert, who was active in the formative period of the state.

Location: Lake County, approximately 10 miles (16 km) southwest of Leadville, within the San Isabel National Forest.

Height: 14,433 feet

Of Note:

▶ The highest peak in the Rocky Mountains of North America;

▶ Highest of Colorado's 53 "Fourteeners" (mountains higher than 14,000 feet).

▶ Highest point of the Sawatch Range.

▶ Second highest mountain in the contiguous United States, after Mount Whitney in California, 65 feet (20 m) shorter than Whitney's 14,505 feet (4,421 m).

**Mt. Elbert
Sawatch Range, Leadville, CO**

Although it was the highest peak in the Rockies in the United States, Elbert is often called the "gentle giant" and considered one of the easiest of Colorado's 14ers to climb. Nevertheless, the South Trail is a 12-mile round trip with a 4,900-foot elevation gain—not exactly a Sunday stroll in the park.

When I informed people of my latest goal, they truly thought I'd lost my mind. "You're crazy if you try to do this," Dad said. "You'll be lucky if you don't die up there." Mom was more subtle but just as concerned: "Please don't do this, Mikie," she implored. But with typical stubbornness, in June of 2003 I began training in earnest for my third mountain climb in five years. However, this one was going to be far more difficult than the others and nearly unheard of for someone who had suffered such a severe spinal injury. My goal was to be ready for the attempt by the first week of August. To my delight and surprise, both Sean and Ryan offered to come along. Although thrilled, I suspected their motivation was out of fear for my safety rather than a desire for a mountain climbing ordeal.

I started by working out at home, graduated to climbing stairs at work, and then hiking increasingly longer distances about four times a week. On alternate days, I did weight resistance work to strengthen my leg muscles, which would always be weaker because of permanent damage to my spinal cord. Accepting this fact of life, I resolved to work all the harder to be in the best shape possible. Doing so had a double purpose because I knew I would grow progressively weaker if I didn't continue working on my strength. With less strength would come more pain.

Somberly, I advised Sean and Ryan that they also needed to work out harder than at any time in their lives if they expected to make the climb without injury. Looking up from their video games, they stared at me in amused silence. Their thoughts were easy enough to read: Silly father, go away, can't you see we're busy? they said with their eyes.

One more time, I planned a 15-mile "dress rehearsal" with a full-day pack. However, in my haste, I forgot one of the most important things—food, a foolish mistake! Nevertheless, away I went one Saturday morning. Things started out well and I reached the Kansas River halfway mark shortly before noon. Taking off my hiking boots, I massaged my feet, lay on my back, and sipped water, watching the leaves of the tall cottonwood trees dance in the wind while singing their beautiful, mournful song. The warmth of the sun felt good against my face, and I began to doze as the wind softly brushed my brow.

Refreshed from a half-hour rest, I started back. With lush Missouri foliage on either side of the trail, I kept a slow but steady pace. As the afternoon temperature rose, the lack of food seriously began to sap my energy. Despite my usual left-side heaviness and growing pain, I maintained good spirits and appreciated the now-familiar sights along the way. Maybe I'll get away with another bone-headed mistake, I thought.

Then, with only two miles to go, a sharp pain shot up my right side. I immediately realized what had happened. For the past 13 miles, I had to consciously lift my left leg in order to compensate for the heaviness. The strain, exacerbated by fatigue from a lack of food, took its toll. My body broke down. The pain intensified with each step until I was literally dragging my left log of a leg until the muscles tore. Eventually, I made it to the car, collapsing into the driver's seat, disappointed and angry.

That night it felt as though someone (me!) had unhooked my pelvis and hip. Every muscle screamed from stretching or tearing from the bone. If I tore my muscles walking on straight terrain, I wondered, what would it be like doing six miles up a 4,900-foot incline? With the trip less than two weeks away, the climb seemed impossible. In desperation, I made appointments with both my doctor and a physical therapist. Pain pills helped, and the physical therapist prescribed modest rebuilding exercises. Fine, but healing takes time, and I was fresh out.

Needing help fast, I turned to an old friend—Reiki. My appointment with Warren, a Reiki Master, lasted an hour. After that, I did Reiki on myself several times a day and sensed immediate improvement. Days passed; the pain began to subside. Although far from well, I could sense healing taking place in my body. Some of my lost confidence returned.

The night before we were to leave for Colorado, I carefully laid out the things we would need: day packs, walking sticks, rain gear, cold weather clothing, canteens, food, gloves, emergency first aid kits, headlamps, batteries, spare batteries, emergency survival kits, and more. I was taking my sons this time, so I needed three times the gear. What had I forgotten?

That night in bed, I stared sleeplessly at the ceiling. This was it. The time had come to find out, once and for all, whether I could achieve the seemingly impossible goal I'd set while paralyzed 30 months earlier. Some might say I'd already proven the point, but it wasn't enough for me.

I thought back to that time, 30 months earlier, when, sitting in my wheelchair staring out the window from the Rehabilitation Institute I vowed to complete this personal goal, which I had set prior to the injury. Everyone thought it was a crazy idea whether or not they said so. In truth, I also found it kind of crazy, especially after seeing pictures of the towering mountain. Although it didn't have the vertical ascents and steep drop-offs of Longs Peak, Elbert was a long and tedious incline into the harsh world of the arctic tundra above the tree line, accompanied by unpredictable and deadly weather patterns. In addition, I'd be pulling what felt like a 10-pound anchor strapped to the left side of my body with each and every step. I still only had roughly 80% of the strength of a normal person my age on the right side of my body and 67% on the left. While far stronger than the day I left the Rehab Institute, was that enough to survive a 4,900-foot incline and descent over a distance of 12 miles? What if I re-injured myself? Or fell? Help would be miles and hours away. And what about the violent afternoon lightning and thunderstorms as well as the horror stories of people being struck by lightning or caught in sudden, deadly snowstorms? Completely healthy people die every year in the Rocky Mountains for these reasons.

Despite these risks, the exciting challenge that the three of us were about to face would stretch our boundaries to new limits. Many people would love such a chance, while others would be afraid to try. My motivation in accepting the challenge was to prove to myself and to everyone with a serious illness or disability that the only limitations are the ones we place upon ourselves. Whether I succeeded or failed, I would always know I'd tried and refused to let circumstances or other people dictate my life. Knowing myself well, I knew I would chastise myself for years if I didn't at least give it the effort.

As I lay in bed counting off the hours and minutes till morning, a poem I'd once read came to mind:

> I would rather stumble a thousand times
> Attempting to reach a goal,
> Than to sit in a crowd

In my weather-proof shroud
A shriveled and self-satisfied soul.
I would rather be doing and daring
All of my error-filled days,
Than watching, and waiting and dying
Smug in my perfect ways.
I would rather wonder and blunder,
Stumbling blindly ahead,
Than for safety's sake
Lest I make a mistake
Be sure, be safe, be dead.

~Author Unknown

While I loved the message of daring and doing, a warm and safe weather-proof shroud sounded awfully tempting about then. But—it was too late to turn back now!

Chapter 19
Touch the Sky

Who has touched the sky,
Who has seen the clouds as they went singing by?
None but the few,
The few who knew,
The sun by its first name.[1]

We loaded a week's worth of stuff into my car and drove to Topeka, Kansas, where we exchanged my small Saturn for a larger rental car and headed to our next stop, my parents' house in Nebraska, to spend the night. As always, it was great to see Mom and Dad, my Rocks of Gibraltar. I was pleased that they were selling the grocery store they'd owned for 35 years and were on the verge of well-earned rest and retirement. Our plan was to leave poor Darby with them, as he was terminally ill with cancer and needed nearly constant care.

Following an early breakfast the next day, we said goodbye to Mom, Dad, and Darby and began the monotonous 500-mile drive toward Colorado. After connecting with Interstate 80 near our old home in Grand Island, the prairies of Nebraska whizzed by for seemingly endless hours until gradually giving way to the arid, desolate high plains of eastern Colorado. We finally overcame our boredom when, just past Fort Morgan, Colorado, the cherished faint blue outline of my old friends, the Front Range of the Rocky Mountains, came into view. At first resembling a low bank of clouds, the line slowly became more distinct as we sped westward down the long black ribbon of the highway until there could be no doubt of the timeless edifices rising ever higher ahead of us. I felt the same rush of excitement I'd felt the first time Cindy and I saw their grandeur when we moved to Colorado 31 years earlier.

After maneuvering through the hubbub of Denver, we began Interstate 70's long ascent into the mountains. At the first crest, a spectacular panorama of distant mountain peaks rising above deep green moraine valleys greeted our eyes.

Late in the day, nine hours after our journey began, we pulled into Leadville, North America's highest incorporated city, at a lofty perch of 10,430 feet. After checking into our motel, exhausted but too excited to sit still, we scouted the area.

Leadville is an old mining town located in the heart of the Sawatch Mountain Range, about 60 miles southwest of Denver. It's surrounded by fifteen of Colorado's 53 mountains higher than 14,000 feet, the backbone of the Rockies. In the 19th century, rugged men with as many struggles as I'd faced made fortunes, lost them, and sometimes gained them back again in these mountains. The area is rich in mineral deposits—lead, copper, silver, and gold—and is pocked with old mines. It was the home of some of Colorado's most colorful characters, including Mary "Baby Doe" Tabor (the Matchless Silver Queen), Molly Tobin Brown ("the unsinkable Molly Brown"), and Doc Holliday, who lived in Leadville after the gunfight at the OK Corral.[2]

We spent our first full day in Leadville sightseeing to give our bodies time to rest and acclimate to the high altitude. We poked our heads into cheesy tourist traps and wondrous rock shops, then sampled the delicious local cuisine. On the second day, we attempted a practice climb of a relatively modest-sized mountain near town. Our trail that day was level for the first four miles or so before becoming steeper until reaching the timberline. Although easy by Colorado standards, the day's climb was vastly more challenging than anything I had done in Kansas! Happily, we strode along the trail, immersing ourselves in the sun-splashed day marked with crystal-clear, gurgling mountain streams and whispering pines.

Just before reaching the turnaround point, we came to a steep incline about 100 yards long. Eyeballing the challenge, I gulped. Uh oh, this is going to tell the tale. If I can make it up and back down this steep hill, I might actually have a chance of pulling off this stunt.

It's funny how sometimes seemingly minor obstacles can be the severest obstacle to achieving a goal because of the limitations we've imposed upon ourselves. After a few breaths ending in a deep sigh, I strode forward.

Silently, I said to myself, "Concentrate on the ground in front of your feet and lift your left foot an extra inch or so with each step." My two homemade walking sticks were invaluable, as they saved me from too many falls to count. With eyes fixed on the trail, I gingerly placed one foot in front of the other until Sean's boots replaced the ground in front of me as he stood at the timberline, admiring the view. Joining him, I stared down the trail, knowing the most challenging part was yet to come. A hundred possible disasters flitted through my mind. Without allowing myself too much time to think about them, I took the first step, terrified I'd lurch out of control and tumble down the hillside. But it never happened. After several long minutes, the ground began to level out.

"Hey, I did it!" I exclaimed with genuine surprise. Although it was just one small hill, it proved something to me. The fear of steep mountain trails I'd been holding inside for months was gone in a whoosh. I allowed myself a bit of smug satisfaction for not having taken someone else's word for what I could or couldn't accomplish. Had I not challenged my fears head-on, they would have tormented me for the rest of my life; I'd never have known that they were nothing but a pack of lies.

With a few ounces of energy in reserve the following day, Wednesday, we took a ten-mile rafting trip down the Arkansas River, leaving from Brown Canyon near Buena Vista. The three of us were looking forward to a lazy, relaxing day. Little did we realize that Class 3 rapids awaited us, which, on a scale of five made for some pretty serious "white water" for a bunch of amateurs.

Our guide was in his first year leading such trips and had us, along with three other adventurous fools, to look out for. I took the left rear seat opposite the guide. The first thing I noticed was that there wasn't a seat in front to grab onto or lock my legs under. "No problem, this can't be that hard," I said heartily.

For the first hour or so, things went well. Our raft glided on the tumultuous, frothy water as we marveled at the towering bluffs bordering the river on either side. I was enjoying the warm afternoon with puffy clouds scattered here and there in the sky when the raft suddenly came to a mass of churning white water. CRASH! The raft smacked the bottom of a trough before lurching upward like a bucking bronco to a crest, then plummeted again into a wall of water that sent a frothy spray high into the air before cascading down upon us. We yelled in exhilaration. Over and over, the raft smashed into the frothing water, its nose completely submerged as water arced around us. It was great to be alive!

Arkansas River Rafting

For a while, the water smoothed before furious rapids appeared around a bend. Uh oh, here we go again. Within seconds, our raft went up, up, up before the bottom dropped out, and it fell several feet, landing with a thud. The nose disappeared again under the water as a wall of water crashed against boulders on either side. This time, the raft lurched to the left and slammed into some submerged rocks, while at the same moment, a wall of water crashed over the right side of the bow, drenching the crew.

The next thing I knew, I was underwater in a raging current. A large boulder rubbed against my right side. Funny to say, but rather than being fearful, I was in bliss. The silent, watery world around me was warm and silky soft. Why hadn't I spent more time in the water all these years? Calmly, I decided to dog-paddle to shore and walk out of the canyon because I assumed the raft was long gone down the river by now. Suddenly, a hand appeared from the surface, latched onto my life preserver, and hauled me into the raft like a carp on a fish line. The whole thing was over in less than 30 seconds, even though the Zen-like underwater experience seemed much longer. Everyone inside the raft was silent in awkward embarrassment, especially Sean and Ryan. Grinning sheepishly, I shrugged and said, "Hey, the water's fine. You guys oughta jump in, too!"

We went through more rapids, but they were nothing compared to the "big one." Several hours later, we reached our take-out point. I felt fine as our raft bumped against the dock. But when I tried to get up, to my surprise, a jolt of pain shot up the left side of my body. Getting tossed out of the raft had pulled all the muscles on the left side of my body. I couldn't lift my left arm above my head, and the pain from the barely-healed injury to my right hip and pelvis two weeks earlier was back in full force.

No one spoke during the ride back to our Leadville motel as the grim reality of my latest injury set in. Fat raindrops splattered against the windshield: only the flip-flop of the windshield wipers broke the silence. When we got back to the motel, I retreated to a corner of the room to be alone with my thoughts, dejected and racked in pain. How can I possibly climb a 14,400-foot mountain six hours from now? I called Mom in Nebraska and, through a cracking voice, told her what had happened. For the past 30 months, I'd been trying to prove wrong the experts who said severe spinal injuries can't be overcome. Doing so was as much for my benefit as well as anyone who has ever faced a serious injury or illness and was told it couldn't be overcome. A freak accident may have suddenly ended my quest.

We turned in early, but before crawling into bed the guys packed ice against my left side. The room became dark and quiet. Gently, I placed my hands on the places that hurt the most, a Reiki technique, and repeated over and over a healing mantra directed to my damaged muscles. I tried to sleep but jolted awake in pain whenever I accidentally moved.

Meanwhile, I suspected Sean and Ryan were having their own doubts. Sean had pushed himself to his physical limit playing football in high school a few years before and had done some jogging in the weeks prior to coming to Colorado. Ryan used to play baseball every summer but never did much hard cardiovascular work and had trained little for the climb. I knew neither of them had any idea of the difficult challenge they were going to face in just a few short hours. My hope was that their youth and strength would enable them to meet the challenge.

This was going to be a massive test for all of us. Beyond the actual climbing, there were other things to fear. "Fourteeners," as mountaineers call them, are dangerous for even the most able-bodied people. What if one of us fell or became incapacitated high on the mountain? Help would be a long way down. A saving grace: Cindy thoughtfully had sent the boys walkie-talkies to maintain communication in an emergency.

Bzzzzzzzzzzzzzzz. The alarm sounded at precisely 3:00 A.M., cutting through our groggy brains like a chainsaw. No one moved in their beds, hoping the noise was just a bad dream, a dream that refused to go away. It seemed only minutes since I'd finally dozed off. The room was icy cold as Sean and Ryan to slowly stir in their toasty beds. "Well, what are we doing?" Sean asked in a husky voice. "Let's get dressed and go to the trailhead," I mumbled, "I'll see how I feel when we get there."

As Ryan and Sean took their turns in the bathroom, I remained motionless in bed, afraid to move for fear of the pain I anticipated was sure to follow. After the final man came out of the bathroom, the inevitable could no longer be avoided. Commanding them into action, I swung my legs over the side of the bed and sat up. To my surprise, the pain, although still prominent, wasn't as bad as it had been only a few hours earlier.

Carefully, I began dressing: support stockings, jeans, rain-resistant pants, two pairs of socks, and a T-shirt under an extraordinary cotton shirt. The shirt came from the Rehabilitation Institute. I had promised them I'd wear it when I climbed a mountain someday. On the shirt was a drawing of a mountain and the words, in ascending order: **positive attitude, achievement, never quit, strength, triumph, perseverance, determination, victory, success.**[3] Although success seemed unachievable at that moment, I needed the positive affirmation.

A light rain coated us on that chilly, starless night as we loaded our gear into the car to begin the ten-mile drive to the Elbert trailhead. We would be taking the lesser-used South Trail. Although longer than the shorter and more popular North Trail, the incline wasn't as steep. Thirty minutes later, the car's headlights pierced a thick black curtain, casting a sliver of light on the road as we approached an empty parking lot. Although there was a road for four-wheel-drive vehicles, we decided to begin walking from the parking lot. It was 3:40 a.m., Wednesday, August 7, 2003, exactly 30 months to the day of my accident. It was also six months to the day since my divorce had become final. The irony was lost upon no one.

Silently, we hoisted backpacks and checked headlamps before strapping them over our ball caps. "Well, what's the verdict?" Ryan asked. "Let's just start walking," I said. "I'll just take it one step at a time. If the pain becomes too much, I'll turn back, and you guys can go on without me." With a quick glance back at the car—our last connection to civilization—we took a collective deep breath and began trudging up the road. Boots crunched against rocks on the heavily rutted SUV road, and day packs swayed rhythmically against rain gear. Small shafts of light from our headlamps danced on the trail in front of us. Rain fell silently on the verdant forest cocooning the trail, carpeting a ravine far below. The damp air was an olfactory delight—a titillating brew of spruce, aspen soil, moss, and decaying vegetable matter concocted in Pan's kitchen, the living earth.

The advantage of traveling in a group quickly became apparent when, during a brief stop, my headlamp fell to the ground and broke into pieces. This would have been a serious mishap had I been alone. As it was, we simply pressed onward with me bringing up the rear, following the other two bobbing lights.

Forty-five minutes later, after crossing an ankle-deep rushing stream, we reached the trailhead. The sun had yet to peek over the horizon, making for a furtive, shadowy world of secrets. Soon, shadows became individual shapes illuminated by the glow of the approaching dawn. It felt good to sit down, have a sip of water, and change our soaking socks. After snapping a few pictures at the trailhead sign, the climb "officially" began.

At the Trailhead

Immediately, we struggled mightily up a 45 to 60-degree incline stretching an entire mile. In an endless battle against gravity, we stretched our arms to latch onto slender lodgepole pines then held tight to keep from falling backward down the hill. After catching our breath, we strained to reach the next tree a few feet higher every time we established our grip.

The incline seemed to go on forever and I'm sure we were all thinking the same thing: if the entire climb was like this, we didn't stand a chance. Eventually, the trail leveled out somewhat and, at the first large flat boulder, we tossed our gear aside and collapsed onto the ground, lungs heaving. Once our strength had returned, we sat up just in time to see the rim of the morning sun peeking over the rim of the Sawatch Range. A dark green, lush floor of a glacier moraine lay far below. To the west, an imposing spine of jagged peaks, reaching toward the heavens, stretched as far as the eye could see in both directions. Lodgepole and ponderosa pines towered above us. The early morning air was as crisp, clean, and fresh as ice water. The sweet scent of pine filled the air.

The wind was calm, and the mountains were as silent as cathedrals, except for the occasional cry of a mountain jay or the chatter of a chipmunk scampering from rock to rock. Overarching it all was an electric blue sky reaching to infinity.

Taking in the surroundings, I gave thanks for my second chance at life. To be in this place, at this moment, surrounded by the beauties of the universe with my sons at my side, was a gift to savor till the end of time. While we all have such moments, too often, we take them for granted. It's easy to forget just how precious each such moment is and that it all can be taken from us in the blink of an eye.

Rejuvenated, we hoisted our gear and set out again. By now, we had traveled a little over three miles, leaving four to go. As the sun rose, taking away the night chill, everyone seemed optimistic. I was holding up surprisingly well with the aid of leg wraps and long johns to keep the strained muscles of my lower abdomen and legs in place. The trail maintained a steady incline stretching far into the distance until it became a tiny line at the bottom of a huge uplift. From there, it zigzagged upward out of sight.

The trees became smaller and less frequent as we climbed higher. Eventually, it felt like we were Gulliver looking down on a miniature forest. Just a few feet higher, no trees were visible anywhere. This was it, the end of the world we had known all our lives and the beginning of one that few people ever experience: Alpine Tundra, where the oxygen is too thin for trees or many other kinds of life to survive. It is populated by plants and animals that many people on Earth never experience.

Here, the weather is unpredictable, primordial. There can be the clearest, bluest sky imaginable but within an hour a raging snow, hail, or lightning storm can emerge. More than its changeability, the energy of being high on a mountain surrounds and engulfs a person. Energy flows through your veins, revitalizing your blood with new life accompanied by the invigorating realization that today is a great day and you are living, feeling, and enjoying life to the fullest.[4]

Going back to the last stand of shrubs, we shed our heavier clothing and hid it in the brush. I also jettisoned my heavy day pack for a lighter "summit pack," which fit around my waist. This was a trick I'd learned climbing Longs Peak four years prior as a way to conserve energy, taking only essential items such as water, a bit of food for energy, and a few emergency medical provisions for the final push to the summit. Especially in my weakened physical condition, the lighter load could make the difference between success and failure.

The South Elbert Trail is considered a Class 1 climb, meaning it is essentially a long hike. However, from the base of a gigantic uplift to the summit, the trail becomes a series of steep switchbacks, some of which require Class 2 climbing—steeper scrambling with increased exposure and a greater chance of severe injury or death.

Sean reached the uplift first, where he waited until we caught up. Looking back for the first time we saw Twin Lakes where we had parked the car, looking more like a puddle rather than a lake. Ahead and above was a jagged backbone of peaks pointing skyward. The precipice of Mount Elbert was hidden. As the sun rose in a cloudless sky, people and mountains alike were warmed by its rays.

Our task was far from easy to accomplish.. After glancing upward and taking a few deep breaths, we began the ascent again. With the exception of the first mile, the trail was the steepest of the day and seemed endless.

Sean led for a while, with me fairly close behind. Ryan brought up the rear and began to lag further and further behind. Sean was doing well, but I was feeling the strain. It reminded me how much more forgiving our bodies are at age 20 than 54.

My climbing poles were invaluable. Over and over, they enabled me to set a position and pull myself upward, preventing me from falling backward. As one switchback led to another, Ryan continued to fall farther behind. He was struggling; I wished I could help him, but my hands were full. Anyway, our individual tests were as much mental as physical.

Finally, I took the lead as Sean's gasps for air became deeper. Suddenly, the trail became even steeper. Without warning, I lost my balance and started to tumble backward. Sean caught me in his arms and literally pushed me forward. Had it not been for him, I'd have gone head over heels backward and, in my condition, maybe all the way down the mountain. My son symbolized for me all the people who had helped me for the past 30 months. While positive thinking and determination are essential, on the trail, it was clear that when the chips are really down, we most of all need one another.

In time, we began to overtake other hikers. As we surmounted one of the countless little rises in the trail, we came upon a group of Boy Scouts and their middle-aged leaders. The boys stood impatiently looking down at their leaders who were sitting on boulders, gasping. We exchanged nods and a few words of encouragement, then moved on with a newly forged sense that we were all in this together.

Slowly, the distance began to grow between Sean and me, as did the distance between Sean and Ryan. While both Sean and Ryan were young and strong, their limited preparation was starting to show. While tired, I seemed to have gained a second wind, holding up well. My assorted pains from the previous day had disappeared. Prior experience had taught me the importance of preparation and pacing oneself. Now, here in the high country, both were paying off.

The two-way walkie-talkies proved invaluable as they enabled Sean and Ryan to stay in touch. Ryan was by now a tiny figure on the trail far below, and I listened sympathetically as Sean urged him onward while trying to lift his spirits. Later, Ryan admitted he was close to turning around if it hadn't been for his older brother's constant support and encouragement. While I'd never thought of the boys as being particularly close in the past, the way they helped and supported each other that day either proved me wrong or showed a bonding experience that would last a lifetime.

As noon approached, the temperature continued to rise while the air became increasingly thinner. Each step became an ordeal that left us gasping for air, forcing us to stop every 50 feet or so to try to catch our breaths. Every step required each person to go deep within and draw upon an inner strength of will. I think Sean and Ryan were starting to understand what I'd meant when I said they would learn things about themselves on the mountain they hadn't known before.

Each time I glanced up from the trail, the summit seemed frozen in place, never nearer. We had been eyeing a point that we assumed was the summit for over a half hour, believing our goal was in sight. Imagine my shock when I realized it was a "false summit" and that the actual summit, now in plain sight, was still far above. A few minutes later, Sean arrived, equally chagrined. Far below, Ryan plodded ever upward, slowly but determinedly.

As I leaned on my poles, gasping, I could almost hear the mountain gods laughing and mocking me. I usually found the Rockies to be a mystical place steeped in spirituality, but now I was mad. The mountain symbolized everything I'd been up against the last 30 months: injury, more injury, job layoffs, betrayal, divorce, and extreme emotional strain. And once again I heard those who told me to be content with things as they were because walking, let alone climbing mountains, was impossible. This was personal, and I was ticked off.

"I'm going to climb this mountain or die trying!" I shouted for all three of us. But more than that, I shouted it for everyone who has ever faced an obstacle in their life and has been told they probably couldn't overcome it. I cursed that mountain using every swear word my father (who was a fine cusser) had taught me. Putting one foot in front of the other, I could almost count the rocks as they disappeared, bit by tiny bit, from view underneath my feet. This was now a battle of will as much as a battle for my body.

Consciously, I instructed my left leg to rise, move forward, and step down. Then it was the right leg's turn. Lift, I told it. Move forward. Step down. As I repeated the sequence over and over again, part of my mind traveled to different times and different places. Then, from far away and long ago, the words came back to me; *I ...think...I...can..., I...think...I...can..., I....think...I...can.* Over and over, I repeated the message from "The Little Engine That

Could,"[5] which I had first heard so many, many years ago. The words were my mantra for the rest of the day.

About an hour later, with the sun now directly overhead, I turned a corner in the trail for what seemed the millionth time, expecting to see yet another rise. But instead of an incline, the terrain leveled off. I raised my head. In front of me was a flat surface strewn with boulders upon which a few people sat scattered here and there. To my right were majestic peaks from distant mountain ranges all below me. Behind me was the trail I'd just come up, winding down the side of the mountain before disappearing then reemerging again, an ever tinier ribbon until finally entering into a Lilliputian, forest-covered valley.

Slowly, the realization dawned on me: This is it, the summit. A short distance later, I came to some rocks and collapsed onto the ground with a thud. A few minutes later, Sean arrived and joined me for a well-earned rest. About a half hour later, Ryan came into view and turned the last corner of the trail. We welcomed him with cheers and applause as he joined us. We'd done it! We had "touched the sky!"

For a while, nobody said anything as we sat on separate boulders sipping water and eating our meager lunch, each person lost in thought. I looked at my sons, men now, exhaustion showing on their faces. Class 1 hike or not, climbing the highest mountain in Colorado, the second highest in the continental United States, is a huge accomplishment for anyone at any age. It's something few people in the world ever achieve. They had shown tremendous courage, determination, and refusal to give up. I was never more proud of Sean and Ryan than at that moment.

Stunning vistas lay on all four sides. Directly to the north was Mount Massive, the second-highest mountain in Colorado, at 14,421 feet. La Plata Peak, the fifth-highest in the state, stood imposingly to the south. In the distance were the collegiate 14ers: Mt. Holy Cross, Mt. Harvard, Mt. Princeton, Mt. Columbia, and Mt. Yale.[7] All were below us. Near the edge of the summit was a small stone wall with a stick protruding prominently upward. The wall marked the official summit point, beyond which was a sheer drop-off of well over 1,000 feet. Behind and far below lay Twin Lakes, where we'd begun our hike six miles and eight and a half hours earlier.

We posed for pictures, rested, ate some more, signed the register, and visited with some of the dozen or so other climbers.

Ryan, Mike and Sean
Summit of Mt. Elbert

After resting an hour or so, we began our descent. It was 1:15 p.m., a late start for the most dangerous part of our journey. Most accidents occur on the way down a mountain. It bothered me that midday had passed over an hour ago—the latest time climbers are advised to start their descent. Nearly every afternoon, dangerous thunderstorms build in the high Rockies, sometimes with fatal results for hikers caught in lightning storms above tree line. It was an experience I wished to avoid.

In spite of the danger, we continued to meet climbers on their way up the mountain as late as 3:30 in the afternoon. When we met a young couple, I cautioned them, "Better keep an eye on the clouds." They seemed unconcerned.

While it would seem easier to climb down rather than up, the opposite is true. Fatigue, combined with maneuvering a steep descent over loose rocks, makes it easy to fall. In addition, stepping downward places constant stress on the legs, knees, and toes. When combined with extreme fatigue, it's a recipe for bad things to happen. Over the next few hours, I fell repeatedly. Fortunately, it was onto my back, or I could have been seriously injured.

After finally reaching the bottom of the huge uplift, the trail levelled off and we could see it stretching far into the distance before

171

winding out of sight like a tiny ribbon. But we weren't out of danger yet as tree-line remained far away. Meanwhile, roiling, ominous-looking clouds were thickening above and around us.

Methodically, silently, we plodded along as the sun crept ever closer to a western rim. Suddenly, from out of nowhere, a threatening rumble reverberated from peak to valley. Seconds later, a flash brightened the ground around us. This time, it was followed not by a rumble but by an ear-splitting crack of thunder. Everyone's heart jumped to their throat. A third lightning bolt slammed into the side of a near peak, followed by a dynamite explosion that crackled in the air as large droplets of rain began splatting all around us. In a near panic, we urged our weary legs to move faster, but the effect was barely discernible.

I wondered: What about the climbers we'd passed going up an hour earlier? There was no time to worry about them; we had our own problems to deal with.

As the rain increased, a small grove of shrub trees appeared in the distance, the first we'd seen in hours. On the double-quick, we pushed forward as fast as our protesting limbs would allow. Finally, we were in their midst. While not out of danger, the trees gave a sense of safety. After retrieving our clothing and the day pack I'd hidden behind a rock on the way up, we set out again against a backdrop of ever-rapid lightning flashes and cracks of thunder echoing off stark mountain peaks.

The further we descended, the sheltering trees became taller and more frequent. Their strength and nurturing wisdom gave us a sense of safety and protection; gradually, our fears began to ease in spite of the sound and fury swirling around us. In time, the storm played itself out. It was just another afternoon in the high Rockies, but for us it was an averted catastrophe. Eventually, we came to the steep first mile of our journey, maneuvering with difficulty through the lodgepole pines. Finally, it came into view—the sign announcing the trailhead. Until now, I'd been nearly pain-free, but once I saw the sign and sat down heavily on a nearby log, it was as though my "free-pain pass permit" had expired.

Suddenly, the full effect of the 12-mile, 11-hour, 4,900-foot elevation gain and descent took hold. I slumped wearily against a willow tree that had conveniently decided to grow behind the log. Despite a ten-minute rest, when the time came to stand up, I couldn't. With Sean on one side and Ryan on the other, they lifted me to my feet, whereupon I leaned heavily against them. Someone handed me my walking sticks. I grasped them to keep from falling, then took a step forward with all the fluidity of Frankenstein.

The last mile was the hardest of the entire day for me. At one point, I went sprawling forward onto my face in the middle of the trail and lay motionless in exhaustion. With Sean's help, I struggled to my feet, pain creeping throughout my body. As had happened just before the neck operation, I felt myself a ball of consciousness floating in an ocean of nothingness. Around 5:45 p.m., with shadows deepening all around, we finally caught sight of the car in the distance. In some ways, it was the most beautiful sight of the day.

Following a celebratory meal in town, we returned to our motel room, collapsing into our beds in exhaustion. Except for me, that was. Sleep was impossible as the pain that had been overridden during the climb got its revenge. All night, I moaned and writhed in pain on the floor. Over the next few weeks, four toenails on my left foot turned black and fell off. It was penance, I guess, for asking my body to perform beyond its normal capabilities.

We left Leadville the next day and, before long, were racing east along Interstate 80 to Nebraska to pick up Darby and, from there, home. Sitting in the back seat, I switched from watching the ribbon of highway slice through the Great Plains looming on either side of the road to gazing with sadness as my old friends, the mountains, receded again from view. Nobody talked much; each person was lost in his own thoughts. Against the steady drone of the motor and the constant vibration of the road, I fell asleep. As the "real" world was replaced by an equally "real" world of dreams, I sank into contentment filled with admiration and love for my sons. Their willingness to take on an extremely difficult challenge rather than veg out at home was not only a testament of their love for me but

173

also highlighted determination and strength of character I'd not previously seen.

We all grew up on Mount Elbert that day and demonstrated an old truth: *it's not the goal in life that's important but the journey*. Even more important was knowing that the only true purpose of life is inner peace that can be achieved any time we want it to be so.

In spite of achieving something I had been deeply committed to for 30 months, it was insignificant compared to rekindling the love for each other that we had almost lost sight of. Without it, we are nothing. It had taken most of my life to realize this simple truth and recover the parts of my soul that had been lost over the years. I regretted the wasted years of holding myself separate from others. Now I knew the Simon and Garfunkel song had it wrong; living life as a rock or an island doesn't avoid pain; it creates it.

The walls of isolation I had created around myself had hurt both me and the people I loved most in my life. No one should live their life as a rock or an island because the only result is needless pain and suffering. I wondered whether Sean and Ryan had figured this out as well. Should I tell them? No. It is better to let them learn it in their own way and in their own time. But in my heart, I knew that, by undertaking this challenge, together we had strengthened bonds that I hoped would last a lifetime. I had ridden with "boys" to Colorado and went home with "men," knowing that, truly, it is love that makes the world go around. At long last, I understood the lesson that the tests placed upon my life over the past 30 months were intended to teach.

Eleven hours later, we arrived back in Olathe, Kansas, and following many hugs, we said goodbye to one another and returned to our separate worlds.

It took me several days to recover from the mountain climb. Finally, hobbling to the computer on mangled feet and an aching body, I fulfilled a long-standing promise and wrote a letter to those who had assisted me during my recovery. I thanked each one for the care they had given me during my darkest hours and enclosed a picture of me on top of Mt. Elbert. However, there was a final message that needed to be conveyed. Slowly, I typed, "Never use the word *'can't'* with your patients because you don't know the level of faith, belief, and determination that is inside that person."

My life sure had been a bumpy ride since starting out as a naïve kid from a small town in Nebraska. I had learned many things along the way about the "how and why" of the universe that changed me forever. However, perhaps one of the biggest takeaways, aside from the importance of love, was realizing how destructive it is to put yourself down or place limitations on what you believe you are capable of achieving. I am convinced this is the biggest impediment to maintaining our right to health and happiness. Don't believe those who claim to have all the answers about what is or is not possible. YOU are in control of every situation, and the only things holding you back are self-imposed doubts and limitations of imagination. If you don't like the rules, make your own!

It took the ordeal of that 30-month period for me to learn and manifest these truths. It was as if God had pushed the reset button in my life in order to wake me up. Some people have said what I achieved was a miracle. If so, it is a power we all possess.

So now I knew. The old fable was true. The secret to life had been there all along, hidden within my mind and heart. The darkest night of my soul was in fact the greatest blessing of my life.

Epilogue

Since this book was first published in 2015, I became aware of new information that provided significant scientific proof supporting the premise of the book: the power each person has to manifest his or her own destiny. Some of this information is detailed in Lynn McTaggart's book, The Intention Experiment (Free Press, a division of Simon & Schuster, 2007).[1] The book contains significant scientific evidence suggesting that thought plays a central participatory role in creating reality. Targeting one's thoughts (e.g., intention or intentionality) produces energy potent enough to change physical reality.

Here is an excerpt from the The Intention Experiment that summarizes its major findings:

A sizable body of scientific research exploring the nature of consciousness, carried out for more than thirty years in prestigious scientific institutions around the world, shows that thoughts are capable of changing everything from the simplest machines to the most complex living beings. This evidence suggests that human thoughts and intentions are an actual physical "something" with the astonishing power to change our world. Every thought we have is a tangible energy with the power to transform. A thought is not only a thing: a thought is a thing that changes other things. (pp. XXI-XXII)

This central idea, that consciousness affects matter, lies at the very heart of an irreconcilable

difference between the worldview offered by classical physics— the science of the big, visible world— and that of quantum physics: the science of the world's most diminutive components. That difference concerns the very nature of matter and the ways it can be influenced to change. Intention is a purposeful plan to perform an action. It is unlike desire, which simply means focusing on an outcome without a purposeful plan of how to carry it out. An intention is directed at the intender's own actions. It requires reasoning, a commitment to achieve the intended deed, and a plan of action to achieve the planned result. (XXV).

For a more complete description of these scientists and their findings, consult L. McTaggart, The Field: The Quest for the Secret Force of the Universe (New York: HarperCollins, 2001).[2]

As Jesus, Gnosticism and New Thought proclaim, we are cocreators with God and anything is possible through **Faith, Belief and Action**.

Following climbing Mt. Elbert in 2003, my story received a degree of publicity, including publication in two magazines, several newspapers, newsletters, and websites. I was also asked to speak a number of times to organizations regarding the role that the services of the United Way played in my recovery. As my story spread, I was contacted by people from all around the nation who were facing challenges of their own, all wanting to know the secret of my success. Their stories tugged at my heartstrings, and I struggled to find the right words to address their individual situations. While each response was different, I always tried to convey four things I felt were important as a result of my experiences:

1. Be thankful for every moment because it all can be taken from you in the wink of an eye. 2. Never give up on your dreams. Anything is possible by letting go of preconceptions and putting faith and belief, grounded in love, into action. It is the secret to miracles.

3. Love yourself and everything in the world around you. We all are one.

4. The smallest acts of kindness may affect the lives of others in ways we never imagined. We all have the opportunity to be angels in the lives of other people and creatures with whom we share this world.

I also felt it necessary to tell them that while the mind plays a significant role in health, the benefits of physical approaches to treating human illness are real and undeniable, and it would be foolish to abandon them in favor of a system based entirely on the mind. "Use every tool in the toolkit," I told them, "and remember 178 that the body is just one aspect of our being, and no matter how perfect it may be, it can't by itself guarantee happiness." Of course, while the physical cure of the body is wonderful, it should never be confused with spiritual fulfillment. Some of the happiest, most fulfilled, and most productive people in the world are those who have what appear to others as limitations. Regardless of whether a person is physically cured from a challenge, nothing can prevent them from being happy and content on the inside. We have a choice of how to perceive every situation and if at first you don't like things, "choose again."

To the Buddhist, an obsession with accomplishing an external thing is an enslavement of the mind that limits one's individual freedom by restricting choices. Don't allow your desire for an external thing to determine how you feel about yourself; if you do, you will never find peace. As a Sherpa guide once told a client who was unable to reach the summit of Annapurna, one of the highest mountains in the world, "A hungry man sees a fruit tree and climbs up the trunk to the top because he thinks the fruit on the lower branches is too easy and therefore not worthwhile. After he struggles to the top of the tree, he finds the fruit to be just the same. He did not regard the whole tree before he began the ascent. Often, what we seek is not ahead of us but actually what we have left behind."[3]

The words are prescient as I have faced more challenges in life, including two bouts of Rocky Mountain Spotted Fever, a torn ligament in my hand, two knee replacements and a broken leg. However, the lessons I've learned in life remain constant: **through faith, belief and action, all things are possible. Never give up on your dreams.**

With these TRUTHS freshly ingrained in my mind, I am reminded of George Bernard Shaw's quote about how brief our time on this planet is and how important it is for us to choose how we devote that time wisely. It goes as follows:

This is the true joy in life, the being used for a purpose recognized by yourself as a mighty one; the being a force of nature instead of a feverish selfish little clod of ailments and grievances, complaining that the world will not devote itself to making you happy. I am of the opinion that my life belongs to the whole community, and as long as I live it is my privilege to do for it whatever I can. I want to be thoroughly used up when I die, for the harder I work, the more I live. Life is no brief candle to me; it is a sort of splendid torch which I have got hold of for the moment, and I want to make it burn as brightly as possible before handing it on to future generations.[4]

The message never fails to lift and challenge me to do more after receiving harsh reminders of how precious every moment is on the stage of life. What choices will you make in your life to reclaim your right to health and happiness?

Notes

Chapter 1, *I think I Can*

1. *The Little Engine That Could*, Copyright @ MCMLXXVI, MCMLKI, MCMLIV by Platt & Munk Publishers. All rights reserved. 1980 Printing.

Chapter Two, On My Way

1. Alan Jay and Frederick Loewe, *"I'm on My Way,"* from "Paint your Wagon", by Paddy Chayefsky, The Malpaso Company and Paramount Pictures, 1969.

Chapter Six, The Awakening

1. *Novena* is the feminine form of the Medieval Latin word, *novenas*, "ninth," which is the ordinal number from *novem*, nine. In the Catholic Church, a novena is a devotion consisting of prayer said (most typically) on nine successive days, asking to obtain special graces.

2. A Catholic devotion to the Infant Jesus of Prague. Copyright © 2002 Infant Jesus website All Rights Reserved. Vancouver, Canada. http://www.mahatmaganghiquotes.com

Chapter Seven, Home Again

1. Frank Sinatra, "That's Life." A major part of the "Sinatra Renaissance" of the late 1960s, "That's Life" reached #4 pop, #1 easy listening, and earned a top 30 position in Billboard's R&B charts. Cashbox listed it at #1 in their R&B listings.

2. Werner Heisenberg (Author), F. S. C. Northrop (Introduction), *Physics and Philosophy: The Revolution in Modern Science* (Great Minds Series) (Paperback).

3. The Heisenberg Principle. In quantum physics, the Heisenberg uncertainty principle states that the values of certain pairs of conjugate variables (position and momentum, for instance) cannot both be known with arbitrary precision. That is, the more precisely one variable is known, the less precisely the other is known. This is not a statement about the limitations of a researcher's ability to measure particular quantities of a system, but rather about the nature of the system itself.

In quantum mechanics, the particle is described by a wave. The position is where the wave is concentrated and the momentum, a measure of the velocity, is the wavelength. The position is uncertain to the degree that the wave is spread out, and the momentum is uncertain to the degree that the wavelength is ill-defined.

The only kind of wave with a definite position is concentrated at one point, and such a wave has an indefinite wavelength. Conversely, the only kind of wave with a definite wavelength is an infinite regular periodic oscillation over all space, which has no definite position. So in quantum mechanics, there are no states which describe a particle with both a definite position and a definite momentum. The narrower the probability distribution is for the position, the wider it is in momentum.

The uncertainty principle requires that when the position of an atom is measured, the measurement process will leave the momentum of the atom changed by an uncertain amount inversely proportional to the accuracy of the measurement. The amount of uncertainty can never be reduced below the limit, no matter what the measurement process.

This means that the uncertainty principle is related to the observer effect, with which it is often conflated. In the Copenhagen interpretation of quantum mechanics, the uncertainty principle is the theoretical lower limit of how small the observer effect can be. *Bridging Science and Spirit,* Norman Friedman pp. 50, 66, 201, 203, 206, 216, 256, 285.

4. Bell's theorem is a theorem that shows that the predictions of quantum mechanics (QM) are not intuitive, and touches upon several fundamental philosophical issues related to modern physics. It is the most famous legacy of the late physicist John S. Bell. Bell's theorem is a no-go theorem, loosely stating that: No physical theory of local hidden variables can ever reproduce all of the predictions of quantum mechanics. Bridging Science and Spirit, Norman Friedman, pp. 34-36. In the early 1980s, Alain Aspect proved Bell's theorem, implying 'ghostly action at a distance,' did in fact appear to be realized when two particles were separated by an arbitrarily large distance. Stated more simply, the experiment provides strong evidence that a quantum event at one location can affect an event at another location without any

obvious mechanism for communication between the two locations. This has been called "spooky action at a distance".

5. In short, he produced two photons by heating calcium atoms with lasers. Then they allowed each photon to travel in opposite directions through 6.5 meters of pipe and pass through separate filters that directed them toward one of two possible polarization analyzers. It took each filter 10 billionth of a second to switch from one analyzer to the other, about 30 billionth of a second less than it took for light to travel the entire 13 meters separating each photon. Aspect discovered, as quantum theory predicted, each photon was still able to correlate its angle of polarization with that of its twin. This meant that either Einstein's ban against faster-than-light communication was being violated, or the two photons were non-locally connected. Because most physics are opposed to admitting faster-than-light processes into physics, Aspect's experiment is generally viewed as virtual proof that the connection between the two photons is nonlocal. Aspect's experiments were considered to provide overwhelming support to the thesis that Bell's inequalities are violated in its CHSH version. The Holographic Universe, by Michael Talbot, 1991, Harper, New York, p. 52-53.

6.   John Wheeler, Does the Universe Exist if We're Not Looking? Discovery Magazine, June 1, 2002. Quantum mysteries, suspects that reality exists not because of physical particles but rather because of the act of observing the universe. "Information may not be just what we learn about the world," he says. "It may be what makes the world." Wheeler relishes the profound and the paradoxical. He was an early advocate of the anthropic principle, the idea that the universe and the laws of physics are fine-tuned to permit the existence of life. For the past two decades, Wheeler has pursued... something he calls genesis by observership. Our observations, he suggests, might actually contribute to the creation of physical reality. To Wheeler we are not simply bystanders on a cosmic stage; we are shapers and creators living in a participatory universe.

7. William James (1842-1920). Considered by many to be America's greatest philosophers.

Biography and quotes on answers Website:

http://www.answers.com/topic/william-James?cat+technology.

Chapter 8, Longs Peak
1. Mike Donahue, *The Longs Peak Experience*. The Long's Peak Experience, 1992.
2. Walter R. Borneman and Lyndon J. Lampert, "A Climbing Guide to Colorado's Fourteeners," 1994, Pruett Publishing Co., Boulder, CO.

Chapter 9. The Dark Night of the Soul
1. Brown-Sequard syndrome (BSS) is a rare neurological condition characterized by a lesion in the spinal cord, which results in weakness or paralysis (hemi paraplegia) on one side of the body and a loss of sensation (hemi anesthesia) on the opposite side. BSS may be caused by a spinal cord tumor, trauma (such as a puncture wound to the neck or back), ischemia (obstruction of a blood vessel), or infectious or inflammatory diseases such as tuberculosis, or multiple sclerosis. Wikipedia, http://www.apparelyzed.com/spinal- cord-injury/brown-sequard-syndrome.html
2. *Que Sera, by Doris Day.* From THE MAN WHO KNEW TOO MUCH (1956)\Words by Ray Evans and music by Jay Livingston.
3. "Quadriplegic. Wikipedia.
4. The New Thought Movement or New Thought is a Spiritual movement developed in the United States during the late 19th century that emphasizes metaphysical beliefs. It promotes the ideas that God is ubiquitous, spirit is the totality of real things, true human selfhood is divine, divine thought is a force for good, all sickness originates in the mind, and 'right thinking' has a healing effect. Although New Thought is neither monolithic nor doctrinaire, in general modern day adherents believe that God is "supreme, universal, and everlasting", that divinity dwells within each person, that we are all spiritual beings, and that "the highest spiritual principle [is] loving one another unconditionally. Wikipedia.

   According to the "International New Thought Alliance." http://www.newthoughtalliance.org, "New

Thought is an ever evolving understanding that all of life happens through us, never to us. It uses the term or word consciousness to further explain the process, often quoting Emmet Fox's statement, 'Life is consciousness,' that leads one to the ever unfolding idea that in order to affect a change in our life, the realm of mind called consciousness must first change.

5. Op. sit., Chapter, 1, #1. *The Little Engine that Could.*

Chapter 10, A New Reality

1. Ibid, Chapter 9, #4.
2. Gregg Braden, *The Spontaneous Healing of Belief*, Hay House, Inc., Carlsbad, California, New York, City, London, Sydney, Johannesburg, Vancouver, Hong Kong, New Delhi, 2008, p.11- 12.
3. Op.sit, Ch. 10, #2. Page 53-56, 142.
4. *A Course in Miracles,* Text, Chapter 27, II. *The Fear of Healing*, page 569.3.10, "Who forgives is healed;" 5. "A broken body shows the mind has not been healed;" Page 570.7.4-5, This is the law the miracle obeys; that healing sees no specialness at all. It does not come from pity but from love. Page 577.2.8; "The only thing that is required for a healing is a lack of fear."
5. Pema Lingpa (1450-1521), was a famous saint and siddha of the Nyingma school of Tibetan Buddhism. He was a preeminent *terton* (discoverer of ancient texts), and is considered to be foremost of the Five Terton Kings. In the history of the Nyingma school in Bhutan, Pema Lingpa is second only in importance to Padmasambhava himself. *The Life and Revelations of Pema Lingpa,* translated by Sarah Harding. 2003, Snow Lion Publications.
6. Michael Talbot, *The Holographic Universe,* HarperCollins Publishers, New York, 1991, p. 57.
7. Gary E.R Schwartz, PhD & Linda G.S. Russek, PhD, *The Living Energy Universe*, 1999, Hampton Roads Publishing Company, Inc. page 12: *According to David Chalmers, in his 1996 book The Conscious Mind, proposed that consciousness, like energy and mass, is a fundamental property of the universe, and exists to varying degrees in all things. According to Chalmers,*

consciousness is a universal phenomenon...If science tells us that information, once released, continues in some form forever...the conclusion is that all natural systems store information in an integrative and dynamic fashion that make them alive and evolving. The hypothesis is that information carried by light is eternal: in all dynamic systems, information emerges, remains alive, and evolves interactively. Systemic memory is universal living memory. Shattering the Paradigm of False Limits, Hay House Publishers India, 2008, p. 53-56.

9. George Carlin, May 27, 1972, Santa Monica Civic Auditorium, Santa Monica, California, released September 1972. Reissued by Atlantic Records, 2000.
10. Deepak Chopra, *"How to Know God",* The Soul's Journey into the Mystery of Mysteries," 2000, Three Rivers Press, NY.
11. Stretton Smith, *4T Prosperity*, 4TProsperity.com, All Rights Reserved.
12. Jack Canfield, Mark Victor Hanson, *Chicken Soup for the Soul*, 1993, Health Communications, Inc., Deerfield Beach, FL, pp. 259-260.
13. Larry Dossey, M.D., *Recovering the Soul,* Bantam Books, 1989, New York, P. 44, 265, a study by cardiologist Randolph Byrd of 393 coronary patients at San Francisco General Hospital concluded that patients prayed for by home prayer groups had significantly better recovery rates than the control group that wasn't prayed for.
14. *Framingham Heart Study*, National Heart Institute (now known as the National Heart, Lung, and Blood Institute).
15. Greg Braden, *The Spontaneous Healing of Belief*, p. 46 -47, 82: The Institute of Heart Math Research Center conducts basic research on emotional physiology and heart-brain interactions, clinical and organizational studies, and the physiology of learning and optimal performance. These statistics are drawn from tan online summary of the communication between the brain and the heart, "Head-Heart Interactions." Website: http://www.heartmath.org/research/sciene-of-the heart/soh_20.htm

16. Doc Childre and Howard Martin, with Donna Beech, *The HeartMath Solution*: The
Institute of HeartMath's Revolutionary Program for Engaging the Power of the Heart's Intelligence (New York: HarperCollins Publishers, 1999): pp. 33-34.
17. Quadriplegia is a symptom of paralysis that affects all a person's limbs and body from the neck down. The most common cause of quadriplegia is an injury to the spinal cord in your neck, but it can also happen with medical conditions. Quadriplegia is sometimes treatable, but most cases — especially those due to injuries — result in permanent paralysis. https://my.clevelandclinic.org/health/symptoms/23974-quadriplegia-tetraplegia

Chapter 11, Waters Deep, Waters Wide

1. Carlyle Hirshberg & Marc Ian Barasch, *"Remarkable Recovery, What Extraordinary Healings Tell Us About Getting Well and Staying Well,"* Riverhead Books, New York, 1995.
2. Jack Canfield & Mark Victor Hanson *Chicken Soup for the Soul,* Health Communications, Inc., Deerfield Beach, FL., 1993, Chapter 10, #12.
3. Glenn Cunningham, Wikipedia. http://en.wikipedia.org/wiki/Glenn_Cunningham (runner)
4. Morris Goodman. *"The Miracle Man",* http://www.themiracleman.org/index2.htm) *The Everyday Miracle of Healing: A Profile of Mother Maya,* by Catherine Elliott
5. Escobedo, Shift Magazine, October 2008 2009, p. 5.
6. Elaine Pagels, *The Gnostic Gospels*, Vintage Books Edition, New
York, 1989, pp 119-126. Eric Butterworth, *The Universe is Calling*, Harper San Francisco, 1993, p. 64.
7. Larry Dossey, MD, *Recovering the Soul*, Bantam Books, 1989, p. 222.
8 Matt. 3:13: New Revised Standard Version, *And Jesus said, The Kingdom of God is in you.*
9. *I am a Rock,* by Paul Simon, *The Paul Simon Songbook*, August 1965. Paul Simon and Art Garfunkel, *Sounds of Silence*, January 17, 1966.

Chapter 13, The Long and Lonely Road
1. Infarctions are a condition in which a localized area of muscular tissue is dying or dead owing to insufficient supply of blood, as occurs in a heart attack. A cerebral infarction occurs when a blood vessel that supplies a part of the brain becomes blocked or leakage occurs outside the vessel walls. This loss of blood supply results in the death of that area of tissue. Cerebral infarctions vary in their severity with one third of the cases resulting in death. Wikipedia, the free encyclopedia.
2. Christine McVie, *You Make Loving Fun,* of the British-American band Fleetwood Mac. Published as the fourth and final 45 rpm single from the band's album *Rumours* in 1977. Wikipedia, the free encyclopedia.

Chapter 14, Strange Happenings
1. *The Orb Project*, by Klaus Heinemann Ph.D. and Miceal Ledwith Ph.D., Simon and Schuster, 2007.
2. Op.sit. The Holographic Universe.
3. *The Secret.* 2006, Prime Time Productions, Melbourne, Australia, page 15.
4. *The Law of Attraction.* "You are the owner of all that you perceive. But you can't perceive apart from your vibration. Feel your way, little-by-little, into a greater sense of abundance by looking for the treasures that the Universe is offering you on a day-to-day basis." Abraham. Excerpted from a workshop in Portland, OR, on Tuesday, June 10th, 1997. http://www.abraham-hicks.com

Chapter 15, The "Miracle" of Healing
1. Reiki. A spiritual practice developed in 1922 by Japanese Buddhist Mikao Usui, which since has been adapted by various teachers of varying traditions. It uses a technique commonly called *palm healing* or *hands on healing* as a form of complementary therapy and is sometimes classified as *oriental medicine* by some professional medical bodies. Through the use of this technique, practitioners believe that they are transferring universal energy (i.e., reiki) in the form of *ki* through the palms,

which allows for self-healing and a state of <u>equilibrium</u>. Wikipedia, The Free Encyclopedia.

2. Chi. Frequently translated as "energy flow", it is often compared to Western notions of *energeia* or *élan vital* (vitalism) as well as the yogic notion of *prana*. The literal translation is "air", "breath", or "gas". Wikipedia, The Free Encyclopedia.
3. To protect the privacy of his family, the name has been changed.
4. Dr. James Grau, a professor of psychology at Texas A&M University. The ability of the spinal cord to learn has been proven in a number of studies, including. *No Dullard, the Spinal Cord Proves it Can Learn,* by Erica Goode, The New York Times, September 21, 1999.
5. Reinhold Niebuhr, *The Serenity Prayer*, 1943.
6. Richard Bartlett, *The Physics of Miracles*, copyrighted 2009 by Richard Bartlett. Astra Books, A Davison of Simon and Schuster's, 1230 Avenue of the Americas. 10020.
7. Ibid, *Remarkable Recovery*.
8. Lynne McTaggart, *The Intention Experiment*, Free Press, A Division of Simon and Schuster, Inc., 2007, p. 143.
9. G. Rein, Quantum Biology, Healing with Subtle Energy (Palo Alto, CA: Quantum Biology Research Labs, 1992), as reported in Benor, *Healing Research*, p. 350-2, and McTaggart, *The Intention Experiment*, pp. 151-152.
10. Ibid, *The Physics of Miracles,* pp. 19-21.
11. Eric Butterworth, *Discover the Power within You,* HarperCollins Paperback Edition, 1992, page 13.12.Elaine Pagels, *The Gnostic Gospels*, Vantage Books, A division of Random House, New York, 1979, xix-xx. "Orthodox Jews and Christians insist that a chasm separates humanity from its creator: God is wholly other. But some of the gnostic who wrote these gospels contradict this: (a) self-knowledge is knowledge of God; the self and the divine are identical. (b) The 'living Jesus' of these texts speaks of illusion and enlightenment, not of sin and repentance like Jesus of the New Testament. Instead of coming to save us from sin, he comes as a guide who opens access to spiritual understanding, (c) Orthodox Christians believe that Jesus is Lord and Son of

God in a unique way: he remains forever distinct from the rest of humanity whom he came to save. Yet the Gospel of Thomas relates (#109 & #129) that as soon as Thomas recognizes him, Jesus says to Thomas that they have both received their being from the same source: '*I am not your master. Because you have drunk, you have become drunk from the bubbling stream which I have measured out…He who will drink from my mouth will become as I am: I myself shall become he, and the things that are hidden will be revealed to him.*'"

13. Internet Sacred Text Archives, *New Thought*, http://www.sacred texts.com/nth/index.htm
14. The Law of Attraction. http://www.abraham-hicks.com. Roger Nelson, Ph.D., *Global Consciousness Project*, Institute of Noetic Sciences, http://noosphere.princeton.edu/
15. *The Secret*, TS Productions, LLC, 2006.
16. Gregg Braden, *The Spontaneous Healing of Belief*, Hay House, Inc., 2008, p.128-129.
17. Eric Schmidt, CEO, Google, Techonomy Conference, Lake Tahoe, NV, August 4, 2010, http://techcrunch.com/2010/08/04/schmidt-data. Collective Unconscious/Collective Subconscious, http://www.kheper.net/topics/Jung/collectiveunconscious.html
18. Claude Swanson, Ph.D., *Life Force, The Scientific Basis,* Poseidia Press, Tucson, AZ, 2010. Subtle energy goes by many names, depending on the culture and discoverer, including subtle energy, od, orgone, prana, chi (Qui or ki), torsion and life force, love, kundalini, orgone, space energy, zero-point energy, aura field energy, energy of thought, energy of consciousness, spiritual energy, life-force energy, ether/aether/eter, vril, energy of intention, and intuition. It may be one or more forms of energy, which do not appear to be within the electromagnetic spectrum. Subtle energy appears to be compatible with the theories of Quantum Physics and may not be equated with Newtonian conceptions of 'force' and 'work'. Subtle energy affects virtually every aspect of space…Any physical phenomenon that passes in the presence of

189

subtle energy gets changed a little because the fabric of space-time has been distorted by it. (p. 49)

19-20.   David Bohm, *Wholeness and the Implicate Order*, (1980), London: Routledge, ISBN 0- 7100-0971-2., p. xv. In the enfolded [or implicate] order, space and time are no longer the dominant factors determining the relationships of dependence or independence of different elements. Rather, an entirely different sort of basic connection of elements is possible, from which our ordinary notions of space and time, along with those of separately existent material particles, are abstracted as forms derived from the deeper order. These ordinary notions in fact appear in what is called the "explicate" or "unfolded" order, which is a special and distinguished form contained within the general totality of all the implicate orders.

Author's Note: In essence, the Implicate Order is the "bedrock" from which the "explicate order (i.e., universe) is created. It is a field of infinite possibilities, omniscient and omnipresent, that contains all the potentiality of everything. The key to creating (i.e., manifesting) these potentialities in the three dimensional world is consciousness. It has similarities to the teachings contained in "A Course in Miracles with regard to God and consciousness.

21. Lynn McTaggert, *The Field, The Quest for the Secret Force of the Universe*, HarperCollins, New York, 2008. Theory that the universe is unified by an omniscient quantum interactive field called "zero point energy" that can be influenced by thought.

22 Lisa Randall, *Warped Passages; Unravelling the Mysteries of the Hidden Universe's Hidden Dimensions*, HarperCollins Publishers, New York, 2005. "A whole raft of remarkable concepts now rides atop the scientific firmament, including parallel universes, warped geometry, three dimensional sink-holes and multi-dimensions."

23. Based on the "Kaluza-Klein" theory, light is really a vibration of the fifth dimension...If light could travel through a vacuum, it was because the vacuum itself was vibrating, because the "vacuum" really existed in four

dimensions of space and one of time. By adding the fifth dimension, the force of gravity and light could be unified in a simple startling way."

24. T. Lee Baumann, M.D., *God at the Speed of Light*, A.R.E. Press, Virginia Beach, VA, 2002, pp 38-32.

25 Brian Swimme, *The Universe Story: From the Primordial Flaring Forth to the Ecozoic Era—A Celebration of the Unfolding of the Cosmos,* Copyright @1992, Harpers Collins Publishers, NY.

26. Albert Einstein Quotes on Spirituality, http://www.simpletoremember.com/articles/a/eins ein/.
I want to know how God created this world. I am not interested in this or that phenomenon, in the spectrum of this or that element. I want to know His thoughts; the restore details.

27. *The Lord's Prayer*, the Bible, all versions.

Chapter 16, Not if When

1. Gregg Braden, *The Spontaneous Healing of Belief,* Hay House, Inc. p. 147.

2. *Recovering the Soul*, Bantam Books, 1989, p. 61, 70.

3. Gary E.R Schwartz, PhD & Linda G.S. Russek, PhD, *The Living Energy Universe*, 1999, Hampton Roads Publishing Company, Inc. page 12-13.

4 Lynn McTaggert, *The Field, The Quest for the Secret Force of the Universe*, HarperCollins, New York, 2008.

Chapter 18, Healing the Soul

1. Mount Elbert is the highest peak in the Rock Mountains of North America, at 14,440 feet (4,401 m), the highest of the fourteeners in Colorado, and the high point of the Sawatch Range. It is located in Lake County, approximately 10 miles (16 km) southwest of Leadville. It lies within the San Isabel National Forest. Wikipedia, the Free Encyclopedia.

Chapter 19, Touch the Sky

1. *The Sky*, by Anita Kerr and Rod McKuen, Warner Bros.-Seven Arts Records, 1968.
https://www.youtube.com/watch?v=Pat4a2P6IHQ

2. Leadville, Colorado, http://www.leadville.org

3. The Rehabilitation Institute, 3011 Baltimore Ave Kansas City, MO 64108.
4. Mike Donahue, *The Longs Peak Experience*. The Long's Peak Experience, 1992.
5. Walter R. Borneman and Lyndon J. Lampert, *A Climbing Guide to Colorado's Fourteeners*, 1994, Pruett Publishing Co., Boulder, CO, p. 18.
6. Op.sit, *The Little Engine that Could*.
7. *Summer of Summits.,* https://infinitegeography.com/2020/07/30/summer-of-summits-mt-harvard-mt-columbia-mt-yale/

Epilogue

1. Michael Newton, Awakening, Fate Magazine, July/August 2013, p. 42. Excerpted from "Traveler's Tale," 2004.

2. For a more complete description of these scientists and their findings, consult L. McTaggart, The Field: The Quest for the Secret Force of the Universe (New York: HarperCollins, 2001).

3. The Buddha's Guide to Dealing with Desire. shttps://www.elephantjournal.com/2017/09/the-buddhas-guide-to-dealing-with-desire/.

4. George Bernard Shaw, The True Joy in Life, Written in a letter prefacing his book "Man and Superman: a Comedy and Philosophy." Man and Superman is a four-act drama written by George Bernard Shaw in 1903. The series was written in response to calls for Shaw to write a play based on the Don Juan theme. Man and Superman opened at The Royal Court Theatre in London on 23 May 1905.

Appendix A
Sources Used in Support of Healing

AUDIO/VISUAL

Active Healing, by Amd Stein Chakra Yoga (video)

Chi King (video)

Soup for the Soul, Public Library (audio)

Divine Dialogue, by Ron Roth

Einstein's Theory of General Relativity and the Quantum Revolution,

 The Teaching Series (audio)

Energy Healing, by Rahul Patel

4T Prosperity, Unity Church (audio)

How to Know God, by Deepak Chopra (audio)

Magical Mind, Magical Body, by Deepak Chopra

Meditations for Inner Growth and Self-Healing, by Joan Borsenko

One Mind, by Larry Dossey, M.D.

Particle Physics, The Teaching Series (audio)

Reclaiming Your Spiritual Power, by Ron Roth

Spiritual Healing Intensive, by Ron Roth

The Body & The Mind, Bill Moyers, Public Library (video)

The Power of the Mind to Heal, by Joan Borsenko

The Seven Levels of Healing, by Jeremy Geffen

Training the Mind, Healing the Body, by Deepak Chopra

The Ultimate Deepak, by Deepak Chopra

BOOKS Science

The Intension Experiment, by Lynn McTaggart

A New Science of Life, by Rupert Sheldrake

Hyperspace, by Michu Kaku

Nothing is Impossible, by Christopher Reeve

Recovering the Soul, by Larry Dossey 232

Remarkable Recovery, by Caryle Hirshberg & Marc Ian Barasch

The Elegant Universe, by David Greene

The Hell I Can't, by Terry McBride, Mesa, AZ, 2003.

The Holographic Universe, by Michael Talbot

The Living Energy Universe, by Gary Schwartz

The Physics of Miracles, by Richard Bartlett, DC, ND

The Secret Life of Your Cells, by Robert S. Stone

The Secret Life of Plants, by Peter Tompkins

The Spontaneous Healing of Belief, by Gregg Braden

Spirituality

A Course in Miracles, by Helen Schucman and William Thetford

A Most Surprising Song, (Exploring the Mystical Experience), by Louann Stahl

Christian Healing, by Charles Filmore

Discovering the Power Within, by Eric Butterworth

Healing Myths, by Donald M. Epstein

In Tune with the Infinite, by Ralph Waldo Trine

Power versus Force, by David Hawkins

Ten Secrets for Success and Inner Peace, by Wayne Dyer

The Dynamic Laws of Healing, by Catherine Ponder

The Far Side of Infinity, by Carlos Castaneda

The Prospering Power of Prayer, by Catherine Ponder

The Seven Spiritual Laws of Success, by Deepak Chopra

The Universe is Calling, by Eric Butterworth

A new Earth, by Eckert Tolle

Science/Spirituality

Bridging Science and Spirit: Common Elements in David Bohm's Physics, the Perennial Philosophy and Seth (Paperback), by Norman Friedman

The Field: The Quest for the Secret Force of the Universe, by Lynne McTaggart, 2002, HarperCollins Publishers, Inc., 10 East 53rd Street, New York, NY 10022.

God at the Speed of Light, by T. Lee Baumann, M.D.

Physics and Philosophy, by Werner Heisenberg

Science and Health, by Mary Baker Eddy

The Eagles Quest, by Fred Allen Wolf

The Secret Science Behind Miracles, by Max Freedom Long

The Wisdom of Carl Jung, by Edward S. Hoffman

The Biology of Belief, Unleashing the Power of Consciousness, Matter and Miracles, by Dr. Bruce H. Lipton Ph.D., Mountain of Love/Elite Books, Santa Rosa, CA 95404, 2005

Others

Chicken Soup for the Soul, by Jack Canfield and Mark Victor Hansen

It's More than the Bike, by Lance Armstrong

Naomi's Breakthrough (20 Choices to Transform Your Life) by Naomi Judd The Celestine Prophecy, by James Redfern.

No Dullard, Spinal Cord Proves It Can Learn, by Erica Goode, September 21, 1999, The New York Times.

Appendix B
No Dullard, Spinal Cord Proves

Left to its own devices, the human spinal cord cannot memorize a Beethoven sonata, solve a quadratic equation or conjugate a Russian verb. No spinal cord, detached from its neighboring brain, will ever win a spelling bee or appear as a featured contestant on "Jeopardy."

But neither is the spinal cord -- the length of nerve fibers, neural machinery and blood vessels that constitutes the southern extension of the central nervous system -- as muc h of a dullard as scientists have long believed. An increasing number of studies demonstrate that far from being a passive conduit, slavishly ferrying information to and from the brain, or a repository of unchanging reflexes, the spinal cord has its own contribution to make.

Spinal cord neurons, researchers are finding, are capable of learning in simple ways, and show changes in response to environmental cues that many investigators interpret as a form of memory. Intriguingly, these abilities remain even when the spinal cord is cut off from the brain. "The spinal cord," said Dr. James Grau, a professor of psychology at Texas A&M University who studies spinal cord learning, "is a lot smarter than you think."

The conception of the spinal cord as an active partner in learning comes from a convergence of work in a variety of scientific disciplines, including physiology, behavioral neuroscience, psychology and physical therapy. Knowledge gained from animal studies of spinal cord learning is already helping some patients with debilitating spinal cord injuries. Bernd Pagell, for example, a German schoolteacher paralyzed from the waist down as a result of a car accident in 1989, has gained new mobility and now walks with a walker, thanks to a novel therapy that grew out of work on spinal cord learning in animals.

New understanding of the spinal cord's abilities is also helping researchers study the biological underpinnings of learning and memory and offering clues to the understanding and treatment of chronic pain.

Those who have championed the spinal cords cause over the past century have had something of an uphill battle. Philosophers and theologians of the 18th and 19th century drew a strict distinction between the lofty brain, considered the seat of the soul, and the lowly spinal cord, capable only of reflexive behaviors. Learning, in their view, required consciousness, the exclusive province of the brain.

To be sure, work with patients with spinal cord injuries indicated that the cord retained some flexibility in functioning after cortical connections were damaged or severed. And researchers periodically offered evidence suggesting that in animals the spinal cord could be conditioned to respond to cues, much as Pavlov's dogs were led to salivate at the sound of a tone. But such studies were often criticized or ignored.

That many scientists are now giving the spinal cord more credit is a result, in part, of sophisticated new technologies for examining the brain at work, and significant advances in neuroscientific research. These developments have shown that the nervous system is much more flexible and responsive to the environment than anyone thought.

"It is now clear from a lot of areas that the whole nervous system changes continually in response to development, to learning, to trauma," said Dr. Jonathan Wolpaw, chief of the laboratory of nervous system disorders at the Wadsworth Center of the New York State Department of Health. "There is plasticity and the capacity for change throughout the central nervous system, and that includes the spinal cord."

Many of the same structures and chemical processes that seem to underlie learning and memory in the brain are present in the lower nervous system as well, scientists point out. NMDA receptors, for example, molecules that receive signals from other cells and are thought to be important in memory formation in the brain, are also active in the spinal cord. And NMDA receptors trigger the same neurochemical changes in spinal cord neurons as in the brain.

Blocking the action of NMDA receptors in the spinal cord appears to interfere with simple learning, according to studies by Dr. Russell Durkovic, a professor of neuroscience and physiology at the State University of New York in Syracuse and by Dr. Grau and a colleague, Dr. Robin Joynes, now at the University of California at Los Angeles.

In studies by Dr. Grau and Dr. Joynes, for example, rats whose spinal cords have been transected in the middle region -- cutting off communication to the brain and leaving the animals unable to move their hind legs voluntarily -- learn to keep one leg raised to avoid a shock, just as normal animals do. But when the injured rats are given a drug that blocks NMDA receptors, they are no longer able to learn the response.

In fact, even learning that starts in the brain changes the structure and function of the spinal cord, researchers are finding. Dr. Wolpaw and his colleagues, for example, have shown that training monkeys and rats to alter the size of a simple reflex -- a tendon jerk -- produces lasting changes, both anatomical and physiological, in the spinal cord itself, and the changes persist when connections to the brain are severed. The same appears true in humans, Dr. Wolpaw said, and may explain why training takes so long for athletes and, in particular, ballet dancers, who execute finely tuned movements with their legs. Such skills, he said, "involve changes at many levels in the nervous system, including the spinal cord, and many of these changes occur gradually."

In the hope of understanding more about pain p perception, researchers are studying changes in spinal cord neurons that transmit pain messages to the brain. By recording electrical activity from pain neurons in the spinal gray matter, Dr. William D. Willis, of the University of Texas Medical Branch in Galveston, and his colleagues have shown that these nerve cells respond intensely not only to sensory signals from an injury site, but also to messages from sensory receptors in adjacent uninjured areas. These hyperactive responses last for some time, Dr. Willis said, suggesting that the spinal cord neurons have been sensitized, a process that looks a lot like short-term memory. "These neurons have learned something, just as much as neurons in other higher-up systems have," Dr. Willis said.

In people who suffer from chronic pain after an injury or illness, he said, the new patterns established in the spinal cord may for some reason persist long after damaged tissue has healed, as the neurons continue to send distressed, but now inaccurate, reports to the brain.

It is in the treatment of spinal cord injury patients, however, that the new wave of research is already paying off. An estimated 250,000 Americans live with spinal cord injuries, according to national support groups. For some, the novel therapy used by Mr. Pagell may offer increased mobility.

Mr. Pagell, a 52-year-old high school teacher, said he was driving his car early one morning in 1989 when he fell asleep "for one second." The ensuing accident left him mostly paralyzed from the waist down, except for limited movement in his left leg and sensation in both legs.

He considers himself lucky, because he did not have to give up his job, as many patients with spinal cord injuries do. "I like to work with young people," Mr. Pagell said.

But he was also fortunate in another way: About six years after his accident, he became a participant in an experimental program directed by Dr. Anton Wernig, a professor of physiology at the University of Bonn.

At Dr. Wernig's clinic, near Karlsruhe, Mr. Pagell was strapped into a harness and, with a specially trained physical therapist helping to position his legs, began to take steps on a motorized treadmill, gripping the bars on either side with his hands. Before starting the three-month program, he was confined to a wheelchair. But as the weeks passed, he was able to walk increasing distances on the treadmill, and at the end of the training he had greater movement and could use a walker, an ability he retains today, four years later.

Dr. Wernig's technique was based on animal studies conducted in the 1980's by two researchers, Dr. V. Reggie Edgerton, a professor of 161 physiological science at the University of California at Los Angeles, and Dr. Serge Rossignol at the University of Montreal.

Scientists had long known that the spinal cord contains groups of neurons that, when chemically activated, generate rhythmic flexing and extension of the legs in an alternating pattern. But no one thought that adult animals with longstanding spinal cord injuries could be taught to activate these pattern generators. The learning of locomotor skills, it was believed, could not occur without the participation of the cerebellum, the area of the brain involved in coordinating motor movements.

The U.C.L.A. and Montreal researchers proved otherwise. Designing a special training program in which experimenters provided animals with partial body support, they trained cats whose spinal cords had been severed in the middle region to step on a treadmill. After three to six months of daily sessions, the researchers found, the animals were able to walk, correctly positioning their hind legs and readily adjusting to the speed of the machine.

What was occurring, the researchers theorized, was a type of activity dependent learning: practicing a specific series of movements provided sensory information that somehow re-educated the spinal cord. But most experts were skeptical about whether such recovery was possible in humans. "There's just been this strong underlying viewpoint that the human nervous system is unique and special, and that the brain was essential for everything," Dr. Edgerton said.

Dr. Wernig's success in Germany, however, is changing many people's minds. In one of his studies, for example, 44 German patients with chronic spinal cord injuries were trained on the treadmill for 10 to 12 weeks. At the beginning of the study, only 6 could walk with a rollator or walker; the rest were confined to wheelchairs. But at the end of the training program, 38 patients could walk unassisted, using a walker or canes.

Dr. Wernig's work is stirring great interest in the United States, not only for the potential it has to increase mobility for some patients but also 162 because scientists hope the training might eventually be combined with transplants of spinal tissue.

Research on spinal cord regeneration is still in its infancy, but experts say one obstacle is that when nerve tissue is transplanted, neural connections are unlikely to reattach in the right places. If the spinal cord could be retrained, however, using the locomotor therapy, it might improve the chances for success of such surgeries.

Locomotor training of the type developed by Dr. Wernig is not yet widely available in this country, although clinical trials are about to begin in five American cities. And researchers caution that the therapy is not suitable for every patient with a spinal cord injury, that not everyone is helped by it and that the benefits vary widely from person to person. They stress that it also involves far more than just getting on a treadmill. "It's not enough to have a treadmill and a harness and suspension, and you hang the patient there and tell him 'Now go!,'" Dr. Wernig said. "You have to apply certain rules."

To be eligible for the studies, participants must have "incomplete" injuries, in which connections with the brain have not been completely destroyed. Experts believe that such patients are more likely to benefit from the training. But in an effort to find out more about learning in human spinal cords, Dr. Susan Harkema at U.C.L.A. is also using the therapy with "complete" injury patients like Tony Scott, who was walking his dog in downtown Los Angeles one Friday afternoon last April when a palm tree fell on him, virtually severing his spinal cord.

The 32-year-old patient, who began the training last month, reports to the clinic three times a week. He undergoes a vigorous stretching routine, then is hoisted onto the treadmill, where he works for about an hour and a half.

Mr. Scott, who jogged regularly and played basketball before his injury, may or may not be helped by the locomotor therapy. But he said: "To see myself up and breaking a sweat is very good psychologically. To be confined to this wheelchair is eating me alive."

Some people paralyzed with spinal cord injuries are gaining mobility. A therapist recently positioned a patient's legs on a treadmill at the U.C.L.A. Medical Center. (Michael Tweed for The New York Times) (pg. F1); A patient working on a treadmill to train the injured spinal cord and try to regain some ability to walk. The therapy was developed in Germany. (Courtesy of Dr. Anton Wernig) (pg. F9) Diagram: "Smart Spinal Cords" Researchers are finding that neurons located in gray matter of the spinal cord respond to environmental cues in a way that may represent learning.

Appendix C
Scripture, Esoteric and Literary Quotations

Scripture Quotations

I Corinthians, 3:16, King James Version: *And Paul said, Know ye not that ye are a temple of God, and that the Spirit of God dwelleth in you?*

Gospel of Thomas, 35.407 & 50.28-30k conflated in NHL 119; and 129: *Jesus said, I am not your master. Because you have drunk, you have become drunk from the bubbling stream which I have measured out…He who will drink from my mouth will become as I am; I myself shall become he, and the things that are hidden will be revealed to him.*

Gospel of Thomas, 45.29.-33; in NHC 138: Jesus said, *If you bring forth what is in you, what you bring forth will save you. If you do not bring forth what is within you, what you do not bring forth will destroy you.*

Gospel of Thomas, Verse 48: *If two (thought and emotion) make peace with each other in this one house, they will say to the mountain, "Move away and it will move away.*

Gospel of Thomas, Verse 106: When you make the two one (thought and emotion), you will become the sons of man, and when you say, 'Mountain move away,' it will move away.

John, 5:30, New Revised Standard Version: *And Jesus said, It is not I but the Father within me who does the works. And I can of my own self do nothing.*

John, 10:34, King James Version: *Is it not written in your law, I said, Ye are gods?"*

John, 14:12: King James Version: And Jesus said: *Verily, verily, I say unto you, He that believeth on me, the works that I* *do shall he do also; and greater works than these shall he do; because I go unto my Father.*

Luke, 17:6: New Revised Standard Version: And the Lord said, *If ye had faith as a grain of mustard seed, ye might say unto this sycamore tree, Be thou plucked up by the root, and be thou planted in the sea; and it shall obey you.*

Luke, 17-20: New Revised Standard Version: And Jesus said, *The Kingdom of God is not coming with signs to be observed; nor will they say, 'Lo, here it is!" or 'There!' for behold, the kingdom of God is in the midst of you.*

Luke, 17-21, King James Version: *The Kingdom of God is within you.*

Mark, 11:22-24, New Revised Standard Version: *And Jesus said, For verily I say unto you, That whosoever shall say unto this mountain, Be thou removed, and be thou cast into the sea; and shall not doubt in his heart, but shall believe that those things which he saith shall come to pass; he shall have whatsoever he saith.*

Mark, 11:24, New Revised Standard Version: *And Jesus said, Whatever you ask in prayer, believe that you have received it and it will be yours.*

Matthew, 3:13, New Revised Standard Version: *And Jesus said, The Kingdom of God is in you.*

Matthew, 5:48, New Revised Standard Version: *And Jesus said, Be ye whole, even as your Father in Heaven is whole.*

Matthew, 17:19-21, New Revised Standard Version: *And Jesus said unto them; I say unto you, if ye have the faith as a grain of mustard seed, ye shall say unto this mountain, Remove hence to yonder place; and it shall remove; and nothing shall be impossible unto you.*

ESOTERTIC AND LITERARY QUOTATIONS

Arthur Lovejoy, *The continuity and unity within the world are a graded, hierarchal spectrum, what Aristotle called the scala naturae, or "Great Chain of Being. Composed of an immense, or..infinite...number of links from the meagerest kind of elements...through "every possible grade" up to the 'ens perfectissimum'...."*

Elaine Pagels, The Gnostic Gospels, p. 144: *Gnostics came to the conviction that the only way out of suffering was to realize the truth about humanity's place and destiny in the universe. Convinced that the only answers were to be found 238 within, the gnostic engaged on an intensely private journey. Whoever comes to experience his own nature human nature—as itself the "source of all things," the primary reality, will receive enlightenment. Realizing the essential Self, the divine within, the Gnostics laughed in joy at being released from external constraints to celebrate his identification with the divine being: The Gospel of Truth is a joy for those who have received from the Father of truth the grace of knowing him...For he discovered them in himself, and they discovered him in themselves, the incomprehensible,* inconceivable one, the Father, the perfect one, the one who made all things. Gospel of Truth, 16.1-18.34, in NHL, 37-38.

Eric Butterworth, Discovering the Power within You: *"The basic premise of the quotes at John, 1:14 (And the Word became flesh, and dwelt among us) is that Jesus discovered his own divinity. He knew that what was true of him must be potentially true of all us. He was inviting us to see in ourselves the same light of Christ that he had discovered within him and realized that we have this same potential within, as did he. What I have done you can do. I have created the window—let us look through it together. Never forget this window, for it is your inlet and outlet to all there is in God.*

Larry Dossey, One Mind: *(p. xxviii): If all individual minds are united via one mind, for which there is impressive evidence, it follows that at some level we are intimately connected with one* *another and with all sentient life. his realization makes possible a recalibration of the self- 239 -centered Golden Rule to 'Be kind to others, because in some sense they are you.'*

Page 211: *A drop of water in the ocean is one with the entire ocean in terms of chemical composition but not in terms of volume and power. Just so, a human may be identical to the Absolute in some ways but not in others. The melding of the human and the divine is the themes of the perennial philosophy, popularized by Aldous Huxley. The perennial philosophy, wrote Huxley, is: . . . the metaphysic that recognizes a divine Reality substantial to the world of things and lives and minds; the psychology that finds in the soul something similar to, or even identical with, divine Reality; the ethic that places man's final end in the knowledge of the immanent and transcendent* ground of all Being. (Rhine, "Psychological Processes in ESP Experiences."3 Page 241: The entire universe may be suffused by love. It may even be possible to detect rudimentary expressions of love, a kind of protolove, in the subatomic domain. As we move from there toward systems of increasing complexity, love becomes more recognizable, reaching its fullest expression in humans, with our participation in the One Mind.

Monoimus (Gnostic Teacher): *Abandon the search for God and the creation and other matters of a similar sort. Look for him by taking yourself as the starting point. Learn who it is within you who makes everything his own and says, "My 240 God, my mind, my thought, my soul my body.' Learn The sources of sorrow, joy, love, haste...If you carefully investigate these matters you will find him in yourself.) (Hippolytus, Refutations Omnium Haeresium, 8.15.1-2.)*

Elaine Pagels, The Gnostic Gospels, p. 134: *According to the Book of Thomas the Contender (138.16-18, in NHL 189), whoever has not known himself has known nothing, but he who has known himself has at the same time already achieved knowledge about the depth of all things.*

Page 144: *This conviction—that whoever explores human experience simultaneously discovers divine reality—is one of the elements that marks Gnosticism as a distinctly religious movement. Simon Magu, Hippolytus reports, claimed that each human being is a dwelling place, 'and that in him dwells as infinite power...the root of the universe (Hyppolytus, REF, 6.9.). However, since that infinite power exists in two modes, one actual, the other potential, so this infinite power 'exists in a latent condition in everyone,' but 'potentially, not actually' (Hypolytus, REF, 6.17.).*

Meister Eckhart: *If it is true that God became man, it is also true that man became God...Where I am there is God, and where God is there I am...To see God evenly in everything is to be a man. p. 216, The eye by which I see God is the same as the eye by which God sees me. My eye and God's eye are one and the same—one in seeing, one in knowing, and one in loving.*

Carl Jung, "Memories, Dreams, Reflections," p. 241: Man can try to name love, showering upon it all the names at his command, and still he 241 will involve himself in endless self-deception. If he possesses a grain of wisdom, he will lay down his arms and name the unknown by the more unknown...by the name of God.

Mansur al-Hallaj (c. 858-922), a writer and teacher of Sufism, the esoteric, mystical tradition of Islam: I am *the Truth...There is nothing wrapped in my turban but God...There is nothing in my cloak but God.*

Charles Fillmore: Jesus Christ Healed: *Ages of thought upon the reality and solidarity of things have evolved in mental atmosphere that has produced the present material universe. These and millions of other concepts are the work of men and not God, as is popularly supposed. However, they all rest on the original God-Mind and can be restored to the perfect law and order of that Mind by those who free themselves from their mental entanglements with materiality and identify their thinking with that of the Mind that is Spirit. "Ye shall know the truth, and the truth shall make you free." We are all in mind related to a great creative Spirit that infuses its very life into our minds and bodies when we turn our attention to it. We have mentally wandered away from this creative Spirit or Father-Mind and lost contact with its lifegiving currents. Jesus made connection for us, and through Him we again begin to draw vitality from the great fountainhead. Ability to pick up the life current and through it perpetually to vitalize the body is based on the 242 right relation of ideas, thoughts and words. These mental impulses start currents of energy that form and also stimulate molecules and cells already formed, producing life, strength, and animation where inertia and impotence was a dominant appearance. This was and is the healing method of Jesus.*

John Milton: *...Celestial light Shine inward, and the mind through all her powers Irradiate, there plant eyes, all mist from thence Purge and disperse, that I may see and tell Of things invisible to mortal sight.*

Plotinus: *No doubt we should not speak of seeing, but instead of seer, speak boldly of a single unity. For in this seeing we neither distinguish nor are there two. The man...is merged with the Supreme...one with it.*

Rumi: *Come, come, whoever you are, wanderer, fire worshiper, lover of leaving. This is not a caravan of despair. It does not matter that you have broken your vow a thousand times, still come, and yet again come.[13] Schrodinger: The earliest records to my knowledge date back some 2500 years or more. From the early great Upanishads the recognition ATMA = BRAHMAN.*

Shankara, Hindu Sage (8th Century): *Though differences be none, I am of Thee, Not Thou, O Lord, of me; For the sea is verily the Wave, not of the Wave the Sea. 15 243 Russell Targe (p. 258): The Flower Ornament Scripture, 100 ce, teaches that here is no paradox in precognition or in communicating with the dead because past, present, and future are all infinite in extent and dependently co-arising. Thus, the future can affect the past— and since our awareness is timeless and nonlocal, it should not be surprising that we can and do experience manifestations of the deceased or communications from the future in precognitive dreams.*

Walt Whitman, p. 244: *A vast similitude interlocks all... All souls, all living bodies though they be every so different... All identities that have existed or may exist on this globe, or any other globe, All lives, and deaths, all of the past, present, future, This vast similitude spans them, and always has spann'd, And shall forever span them and compactly hold and enclose them.*

William Blake: See a world in a grain of sand and heaven in a wild flower. Hold infinity in the palm of your hand and eternity in an hour." [18]

Bibliography

A Catholic devotion to the Infant Jesus of Prague. Copyright © 2002 Infant Jesus website All Rights Reserved. Vancouver, Canada.

Bartlet, Richard. The Physics of Miracles, copyrighted 2009 by Richard Bartlett. Astra Books, A Division of Simon and Schuster's, 1230 Avenue of the Americas. 10020.

Blake, William. (n.d.). BrainyQuote.com. Retrieved December 28, 2014, from BrainyQuote.com Web site: http://www.brainyquote.com/quotes/quotes/w/william bla150124.html

Bohm, David, Wholeness and the Implicate Order, Routlege Classics, New York, 2002.

Borneman, Walter R. and Lampert, Lyndon J., A Climbing Guide to Colorado's Fourteeners, by, 1994, Pruett Publishing Co., Boulder, CO.

Braden, Greg. The Spontaneous Healing of Belief, Shattering the Paradigm of False Limits, Hay House, Inc., Carlsbad, California, New York, City, London, Sydney, Johannesburg, Vancouver, Hong Kong, New Delhi, 2008.

Butterworth, Eric. Discover the Power within You, HarperCollins Paperback Edition, 1992. Butterworth, Eric, The Universe is Calling, HarperCollins Publishers, 10 East 53rd Street, New York, 10022, 1993.

Canfield, Jack, Mark Victor Hanson Chicken Soup for the Soul, 1993, Health Communications, Inc., Deerfield Beach, FL. Collective Unconscious/Collective Subconscious, http://www.kheper.net/topics/Jung/collective_unconscious.html.

Childre, Doc and Martin, Howard Martin, with Donna Beech, The HeartMath Solution: The Institute of HeartMath's Revolutionary Program for Engaging the Power of the Heart's

Intelligence (New York: HarperCollins Publishers, 1999). http://www.framinghamheartstudy.org/about/history.html

Chopra, Deepak. How to Know God, The Soul's Journey into the Mystery of Mysteries, 2000, Three Rivers Press, NY.

Glenn Cunningham, Wikipedia.
http://en.wikipedia.org/wiki/Glenn_Cunningham_(runner)

Dossey, Larry, M.D. Recovering the Soul, Bantam Books, 1989, New York.

Donahue, Mike, The Longs Peak Experience, 1992.

4T Prosperity, by Stretton Smith. 4TProsperity.com. Felder, Gary, Spooky Action at a Distance, An Explanation of Bell's Theorem, Copyright (c) 1999, http://www4.ncsu.edu/unity/lockers/users/f/felder/public/kenny/pape rs/bell.htm. 168

Goodman, Morris, "The Miracle Man,"
http://www.themiracleman.org/index2.htm.

Carlin, George, Class Clown. 1972. Reissued by Atlantic Records, 2000.

Harding, Sarah. The Life and Revelations of Pema Lingpa, translated by Sarah Harding. 2003, Snow Lion Publications.

Heisenberg, Werner, Physics and Philosophy: The Revolution in Modern Science (Great Minds Series) (Paperback). F. S. C. Northrop (Introduction)

Hirshberg Carlyle, & Barasch Marc Ian, "Remarkable Recovery, What Extraordinary Healings Tell Us About Getting Well and Staying Well," by, Riverhead Books, a Division of Penguin Group, New York, 1995.

Institute of HeartMarh Research Center. Doc Childre and Howard Martin, with Donna Beech, The HeartMath Solution. New York: HarperCollins Publishers, 1999: Institute of HeartMath Research Center. Website:
http://www.heartmath.org/research/sciene-ofthe heart/soh_20.html.

Jay, Alan & Loewe, Fredereck, "I'm on My Way," from "Paint your Wagon," by Paddy Chayefsky, The Malpaso Company and Paramount Pictures, 1969.

Leadville, Colorado, http://www.leadville.org. Life Force,

The Scientific Basis, by Claude Swanson, Ph.D., Poseidia Press, Tuscon, AZ, 2010.

Lipton, Bruce H., PhD. The Biology of Belief, Unleashing the power of Consciousness, Matter and Miracles, Mountain of Love/Elite Books, Santa Rosa, CA 95404, 2005. http://noosphere.princeton.edu/terror.html Stark effect:

The shift in energy levels caused by an external electric field is called the Stark effect. http://www.physics.csbsju.edu/QM/H.10.html. Mahatma Gandhi Quotes. http://www.mahatmaganghiquotes.com McTaggert, Lynne. The Field:

The Quest for the Secret Force of the Universe, 2002, by HarperCollins Publishers, 10 East 53rd Street, New York, NY 10022.

Nelson, Roger D., "The Global Consciousness Project" (GCP), (EGG Project), Princeton University. http://en.wikipedia.org/wiki/Global_Conscio

Niebuhr, Reinhold, Serenity Prayer, 1943. "No Dullard, the Spinal Cord Proves it Can Learn," by Erica Goode, The New York Times, September 21, 1999.

Northrop, F.S.C. (Introduction). Heisenberg, Werner, Physics and Philosophy: The Revolution in Modern Science (Great Minds Series) (Paperback). Orbs. http:psychicinvestigators.net Pagels, Elaine,

The Gnostic Gospels, Vintage Books Edition, a Division of Random House, Inc., New York, 1989.

Radin, Dean, PhD, "Emerging Worldviews, The Enduring Enigma of the UFO," Shift Magazine, Winter 2008-2009.

Robinson, James M. ed., The Gospel of Thomas, from The Nag Hammadi Library, San Francisco: Harper, San Francisco, 1990.

Sacred Text Archives, "New Thought," http://www.sacred-texts.com/nth/index.htm

Schwartz, Gary E.R. PhD & Linda G.S. Russke, PhD, The Living Energy Universe,1999, Hampton Roads Publishing Company, Inc. September 11 2001: Exploratory and Contextual Analyses.

Schrodinger, Erwin, My View of the World, Woodbridge, CT: Ox Bow Press; 1983.

Shaw, George Bernard, The True Joy in Life, "Man and Superman: a Comedy and Philosophy.

Smith, Stretton. 4T Prosperity, 4TProsperity.com. Stark effect: The shift in energy levels caused by an external electric field is called the Stark effect. http://www.physics.csbsju.edu/QM/H.10.html.

Swanson, Claude, PhD, Life Force, The Scientific Basis, Poseidia Press, Tuscon, AZ, 2010.

Swimme, Brianne, The Universe Story: From the Primordial Flaring Forth to the Ecozoic Era--A Celebration of the Unfolding of the Cosmos, Copyright @1992, Harpers Collins Publishers, NY.

Talbot, Michael, The Holographic Universe, 1991, HarperCollins, Publishers, New York.

The Intention Experiment, McTaggart, Lynne, Free Press, a Division of Simon & Schuster, 2007.

Whitman, Walt, The Complete Poems, New York, Penguin Classics; 2004.

Wikipedia, The Free Encyclopedia:

    x God x Glenn Cunningham

    x Quantum Entanglement

x Quadriplegic x Reiki

x Chi

x Mt. Elbert

Songs/Audio

Class Clown, by Carlin, George, 1972. Reissued by Atlantic Records, 2000.

I am a Rock, by Paul Simon, The Paul Simon Songbook, August 1965. Paul Simon and Art Garfunkel, Sounds of Silence, January 17, 1966.

Paint your Wagon, by Alan Jay and Frederick Loewe, "I am on my Way," by Paddy Chayefsky, The Malpaso Company and Paramount Pictures, 1969.

Que Sera Sera, by Doris Day. From THE MAN WHO KNEW TOO MUCH, 1956. Words by Ray Evans and music by Jay Livingston.

That's Life, by Frank Sinatra. 1966 album by Frank Sinatra, supported by a studio orchestra arranged and conducted by Ernie Freeman.

The Little Engine That Could, Copyright @ MCMLXXVI, MCMLKI, MCMLIV by Platt & Munk Publishers. All rights reserved. 1980 Printing.

Who Has Touched the Sky, by Rod McKuen, "The Sky," 1967.

You Make Loving Fun, by Christine McVie, Fleetwood Mac, Rumours, 1977.

About the Author

Michael L. McCord is an author, motivational speaker, educator, and lecturer. He was born in 1949 at Fairbury Nebraska, to Lester and Jean (Nicholson) McCord. He grew up in Nelson, Nebraska and has resided in the Kansas City area since 1986. He is the divorced father of Sean and Ryan McCord.

In 1972, he received a Bachelor of Science Degree in Business Administration from Kearney State College and in 1979 a Master of Business Administration Degree from the University of Nebraska at Kearney. Since 1972, he has held management positions in commercial lending, urban redevelopment, commercial mortgage banking, real estate lending, environmental due diligence and commercial real estate appraising/review appraising. He retired from the Department of Housing and Urban Development (HUD) in 2020.

Honors include:

- *Outstanding Young Men of America,* 1980 edition.
- *Housing Leadership A*ward, The Housing Group of Nebraska, 1981.
- *Innovative Programs Award,* The Department of Housing and Urban Development, 1983. In recognition of an innovative, collaborative agreement between Community Development offices in Grand Island, Lincoln and Omaha to create a home rehabilitation program available to low and moderate-income persons throughout the state of Nebraska.
- *Community Service Award,* Bank of America, 2000.
- *Inspiration Award*, Mahaffie School, 2003.
- *Friend of Youth*, 2004, the Olathe School District, "For his six years of service as a mentor for youths in need."

Mike was a spokesperson for the United Way of Kansas Citsy from 2002 through 2006. In 2004, he was both a chaplain at Unity Church of Overland Park and formed its Green Team in 2004, which lasted until 2020.

In 2008, he co-founded Unity Worldwide Ministries EarthCare program and remains its Team Leader. He facilitated the symposium, "Awakening the Dreamer, Changing the Dream," and in 2015 developed "Awakening the Dreamer through Unity."

Mike has been a mentor for the Christopher Reeve Foundation since 2011.

From 2017-2022 he was on the Board and Secretary of The Whole Person, whose mission is to improve the lives of people with disabilities.

Mike publishes the *EarthCare Connections* newsletter and is a regular contributor to Unity Worldwide Ministries, *Unity Partners* newsletter.

Finally, indicative of his broad range of interests, Mike has been a Field Investigator for the Mutual UFO Network (MUFON) since 2011.

Website:
http://www.miraclesonestepatatime.com
Also by Michael L. McCord

Books:

- The McCord Saga, 1996.
- The Kindness of God: How God Cares for Us, 2006 by Paul Robb.
  Contributing chapter: God, What Am I Going to do?
  www.amazon.com

Magazines:

- *Thankful for Every Moment,* The Daily Word, Unity Worldwide Ministries, March 2004.
  (www.unity.org).
- *Not If, When,* Positive Thinking magazine, Nov/Dec 2005; www.positivethinkingmag.com.

Newsletters:

- *Believe You Can,* United Way Success Stories, April 1, 2004,
  http://kcunitedway.org/if_you_believe.htm.
- *Thankful for Every Moment,* Yes! For KC, "Stories that Touch, *M*ove and Inspire,"
  Institute
  for Noetic Sciences Newsletter, Volume 1, July 2004.
- *Touch the Sky,* **Evolving in Consciousness** newsletter,Whole Life Center, Karen Harrison,
  http://www.karenharrison.net; December 31, 2012.

Newspapers

- *Duo Gives Hope to Others,* Olathe Daily News, October 4, 2001.
- *Moral of Olathe Man, Never Give Up,* Kansas City Star, December 6, 2001.
- *Never Give Up,* Energy Newsletter, Kiev, Ukraine, September 2003.
- *From Quadriplegic to Mountain Climber,* Hastings Daily Tribune, May 8, 2004.

Educational Courses/Workshops:

Awakening the Dreamer, Changing the Dream; The Pachamama Alliance,
(https://www.pachamama.org). Creating an environmentally sustainable, spiritually fulfilling,
socially just world. Facilitator, 2007-2015.

- **Healing and Wholeness,** a six week on-line course. Friends of Unity, Plymouth, MI,
  January 2021. **https://www.friendsofunity.org/**.

www.ingramcontent.com/pod-product-compliance
Lightning Source LLC
Chambersburg PA
CBHW051513120626
46551CB00012B/898